HOUSE DESIGN

A CLASSROOM MANUAL

by

ALICE WAUGH
Goleta, California

Burgess Publishing Company
426 South Sixth Street • Minneapolis, Minn. 55415

Copyright © 1955 by Alice Waugh
All rights reserved
Printed in the United States of America
Standard Book Number 8087-2304-9

13th Printing 1971

Foreword

In recent years a marked increase in home ownership has been accompanied by changes in the way houses are produced. Large scale commercial building of entire neighborhoods and the factory prefabrication of houses seem to be taking the place of individual building enterprises.

These changes have not altered the basic fact that the buying of a house still calls for good judgment on the part of the consumer. Women as well as men need to know what constitutes a good plan, and how to recognize good design in the exterior, whether they buy a tract house or build on their own.

The course for which this book was written is intended to help the student prepare for her own future, which probably includes family life and home ownership. A series of exercises in analyzing and evaluating plans develops the kind of good judgment that will be needed when a house is built or purchased.

These exercises in the use of space progress from small simple plans to larger, more complicated ones, They cover several aspects of planning, in relation to family life, the choice and best use of the site, and the relation of the house to the climate. They are based on the belief that we learn by doing; that drawing plans, even in a simple way, is more useful in the development of good judgment than endless lectures and reading on what a house should be.

The study of good design in relation to the exterior of the house is covered in a separate chapter and is also involved in each problem in planning, through the drawing of exterior elevations to go with the plans. The use of current magazines on building keeps the problems in touch with new developments in design and planning.

The technical side of building, such as construction, plumbing, and the like, is not included because such highly specialized work must be done by experts, and cannot be mastered by the layman in a few easy lessons. Besides, changes and developments in these fields are taking place so rapidly that anything written about them is likely to be out of date by the time it is printed.

This course in planning a house is intended to help the student to cooperate with an architect when and if she becomes involved in the building of a house; it does not in any way pretend to enable her to get along without professional help in so important an undertaking.

The historic background of the American house is dealt with, not in terms of copying the houses of the past, but as a part of general cultural development and the enrichment of life. For those who will some day face the problem of building or buying a house, the practical benefits of a course in house planning is obvious. But even if one never builds a house, the study of a subject so closely related to human life is not wasted, for it widens one's horizons and opens new fields of interest and enjoyment.

Table of Contents

CHAPTER			Page
1	-	Buying a Ready-built House	1
2	-	Planning to Build	7
3	-	Drawing the Exterior	19
4	-	Planning the Kitchen	22
5	-	A House Should Fit the Family	26
6	-	A House Should Fit the Site	36
7	-	A House Should Fit the Climate	43
8	-	Two-story Houses	48
9	-	Story-and-a-half Houses	54
10	-	Remodeling an Old House	58
11	-	An Architect Can Help You	63
12	-	Historic Design in Houses	67
13	-	The Problem of Taste	86
INDEX			91

Chapter I
Buying a Ready-built House

"And strange it is to think how building do fill my mind and put out all other things out of my thoughts."
                                                            Samuel Pepys

When the time comes for you to acquire a house you will first have to decide whether to buy an old one or a new one. If you choose the latter, the next choice lies between buying a commercially built house or building your own. In cities and larger towns many houses are put up by large-scale commercial builders. These are sometimes called "tract" or "development" houses. It is easy to see why they usually cost less than individually built houses. Large-quantity buying, standardized parts, and efficient techniques and use of labor, all promote economy. Many commercially built houses are prefabricated, either wholly or in part.

A great advantage in buying a ready-built house is that you know exactly how you stand financially. The purchase price, the down payment, and the monthly mortgage payments, are clearly stated. On the other hand, the cost of an owner-built house is less certain, until the final bill has been received.

In addition, the tract house, or its duplicate, in the form of a model house, is in actual existence, for you to look at and walk around in. It takes considerable imagination, when you build on your own, to visualize the finished house from the drawings on paper. A ready-built house, in addition to giving you the most house for your money, will save you time and effort. All you have to do is to choose the right house and sign the mortgage.

There is a world of meaning, however, in that phrase, "choose the right house". Looking through an actual house in a development is easier, of course, than wrestling with building problems yourself, but if you are to make a wise choice you will need good judgment in regard to the plan, and some understanding of quality in materials and workmanship. Since amortized mortgages are often made to extend over a period of 20 or more years, you may be spending almost one-third of your lifetime paying for your house.

So important a purchase calls for preparation on your part. Buying a tract house is not simply a matter of paying more for a better house. There are good and bad buys in every price range, and you must know the difference between them.

At their best, commercially built houses come close to the owner-built sort. They are designed by competent architects who understand the needs of family life, and are built by conscientious builders who try to give sound durable construction and as much space as possible for the money.

If the enterprise is large enough, the entire neighborhood is planned, with provision for shopping and recreation centers, schools and playgrounds. Streets are laid out to avoid hazardous crossings for children on their way to school, and heavy traffic is routed to bypass the residential areas. The oppressive monotony of rows of identical or similar houses is relieved by varying the position of the houses on the lots and by the use of curving streets that limit the view from any one spot. Some builders offer a choice of several plans and exterior designs, thus creating some variety in the appearance of the neighborhood.

At the other end of the scale, commercially built houses may be flimsy little boxes crowded close together on tiny treeless patches of land. A serious objection to such developments is the fact that they do not have large enough lots, either for privacy and comfortable living, or for future expansion. Their appearance cannot be improved by planting, for there is no room for it. If you drive through an older neighborhood you will see that any house, no matter how old-fashioned or even badly designed it may be, can be made to look better if it is surrounded by enough space for lawns, trees, and shrubbery.

Another handicap of these crowded developments is the threat of deterioration that hangs over them. Owners who cannot take pride in their houses are likely to neglect them. Ambitious families do not set up their lifetime homes in such neighborhoods, but sell and move away as soon as they can afford to do so.

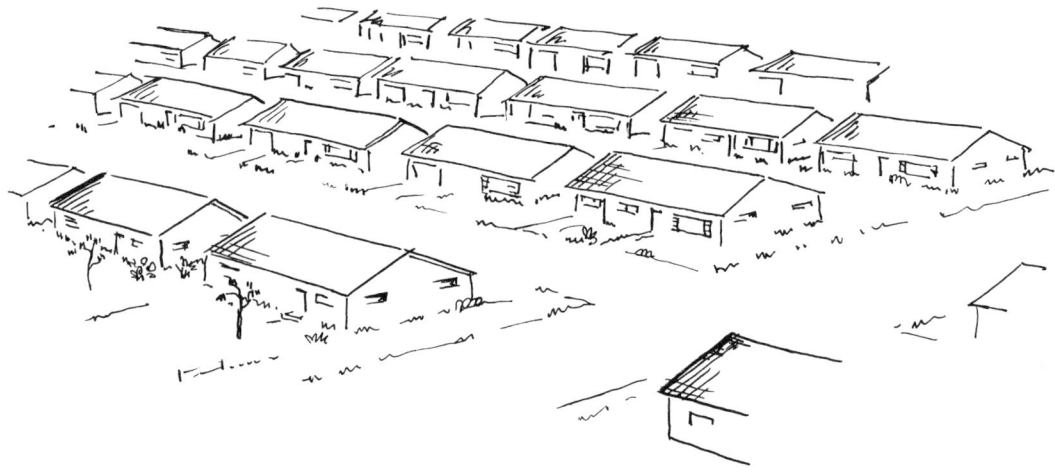

Tract houses at their worst.

Still another danger sometimes encountered in buying a speculative house is that its construction may be skimped. Attractive selling features like electric dish-washers may divert the buyer's attention from the use of cheaper materials and methods of building. Faults in construction are not easily detected in a new house, but they take their toll, in a few years, in high repair bills and unduly rapid depreciation in the value of the house.

The reputation of the construction company is of the greatest importance if you buy a ready-built house. A well-established builder is not likely to endanger his prestige by selling poorly built houses. The average untrained person is not always able to judge the construction of a finished house. It is wise, if there is any doubt, to employ a disinterested builder or architect to look over the house, and to read the specifications. It might also help to visit some of the same builder's earlier tracts, to see how well his houses have stood the tests of time, use, and weather.

Model houses play an important part today in the selling of prefabricated and other commercially built houses. When you buy a house, your decision may be based chiefly on what you see in the models. For that reason you will need to know how to look at them. It is a good idea to take along a tape measure or folding ruler, when you visit a model house, so that you may see for yourself just how large (or how small) the rooms are. Measure also the height of the ceiling, the size of the closets, and the wall spaces in relation to the standard sizes of furniture.

Certain devices used in furnishing model houses may disguise their faults. Sometimes very small rooms are artfully furnished with small-scaled furniture, and not really enough of it for comfortable living, to make them look larger than they really are. Unless you look for such things, you may not notice until you move your own furniture in, that the rooms are not large enough.

In the living room, count the number of comfortable seats provided. There should be enough for your own family, plus a couple of extra chairs for visitors. It is wise to carry with you a list of sizes of the furniture you have, and to check the areas where you will use them, to see if your things will fit. An attractive dining alcove set up for three won't mean much to you, if there are five in your family, and no room for two more chairs.

In the bedrooms, also, measure the furniture. A striking color scheme and unusual accessories may keep you from noticing that it contains two studio couches instead of full-size twin beds. They may look very well, but you would not want to sleep on them every night of your life. If a very small bedroom is furnished as a baby's room, make sure that it will hold full size furniture, for babies have a way of growing up to be full-size adults.

In addition to checking the sizes, study all samples of construction and materials that are exhibited, and look for the brand names of materials and equipment.

When you have a choice of houses in several neighborhoods, you will weigh a number of factors before you decide. First, the general character of the tract should be good. Low ground near a river, for instance, will probably be flooded in wet seasons. Factories, if they are too close, may spoil the neighborhood with smoke and odors. Highways and railroads too near will make a noisy neighborhood. Other things to be looked into are fire and police protection, and transportation facilities.

If your children are small, the location and quality of the schools is of first importance. The kind of people who live in the neighborhood should also be determined. A family of adults enjoys a more mobile social life, but the parents of young children are dependent in many ways on their neighbors. Life is more pleasant if the parents of your children's playmates are also congenial friends of yours.

As industries spread out from cities into the countryside, residential developments usually grow up nearby. Your choice of a neighborhood may be limited to those which allow the working members of the family to get to their jobs without a long ride across the city.

An objection sometimes made to commercially built houses is that they must meet average needs rather than those of any one particular family. Since they must sell quickly in order to make a profit for the builder, many of them are planned to follow ideas that are currently liked by the largest number of customers, even if they are not very good ideas. Picture windows on the front of the house are an example of a popular idea that is not a good one.

Exterior designs, also, are made to please the greatest number of buyers. Some builders seem to have a low opinion of the taste of their potential customers, for they dress up their houses with faddish touches, such as incongruous mixtures of materials, varied colors in bricks and roofing, and eccentric entrances. In spite of all these objections, a tract house, chosen with discrimination, may be your best buy if you lack the interest, time, and money to build on your own.

In a commercially built house the arrangement of the interior space is only one of a number of factors that influence your choice. The plan you like best may be too costly, or in an unsuitable neighborhood, while a house with a less desirable plan may please you in other ways.

There are certain things, however, that we ought to demand of any plan, such as rooms that are large enough to hold standard size furniture, adequate storage space, and a well-arranged kitchen. Other needs are enough windows to provide ample light and air, privacy from the street and neighbors, and also some privacy for individual members of the family.

The prefabrication of houses, that is, the construction of the house at the factory, leaving only the work of setting up to be done on the site, has been developing for a number of years. It has had various obstacles to overcome, among them the general belief that prefabrication always meant flimsy, cheap construction. As the quality of prefabricated houses has improved, they have been more widely accepted. The factory prefabrication of parts of the house, such as doors and windows and their frames, kitchen cabinets, heating units, and the like, won public acceptance early in the century. Perhaps another generation will consider prefabricated houses as standard, and on-site building the exception.

In Figure 2, you will find several arrangements of space that are often used in tract houses of small size and low cost. They are economical because of their size, compact rectangular shape, and simple arrangement. Other favorable comment might be that the basic division of space is logical, that is, the bedrooms and bath are close together, and the more public area, the living and dining spaces, and the kitchen, lie in a convenient relationship to each other. Also, the principal rooms are on corners, where they may have windows on two sides. In each house the kitchen allows an efficient arrangement of equipment.

Houses of such small size cannot be judged by the standards that are used for larger, more costly houses. They are adequate for families of two or three persons, provided that the rooms are large enough and that there is a reasonable amount of storage space. Even in these small houses, however, some arrangements of space are better than others. In plan A, for instance, traffic lines cut through the center of the living room and the bedrooms lack privacy because their doors open into the living room. Two doors to the bath can be a source of inconvenience and friction in family life.

These faults have been reduced in plan B, by the addition of a small central hall, and by changing the position of the front door. The extra space needed for the hall is well worth its cost because of the convenience it adds to the plan. A new fault has appeared, however, in the fact that you can see directly into the bathroom from the living room.

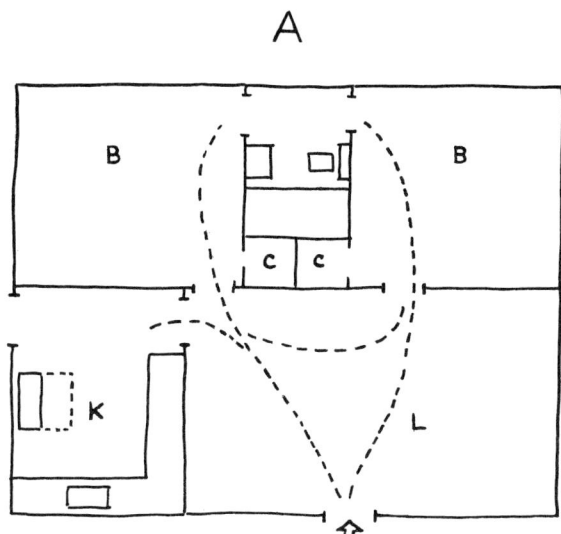

Faults: Many traffic lines in living room; lack of privacy for bedrooms; two doors into bathroom.

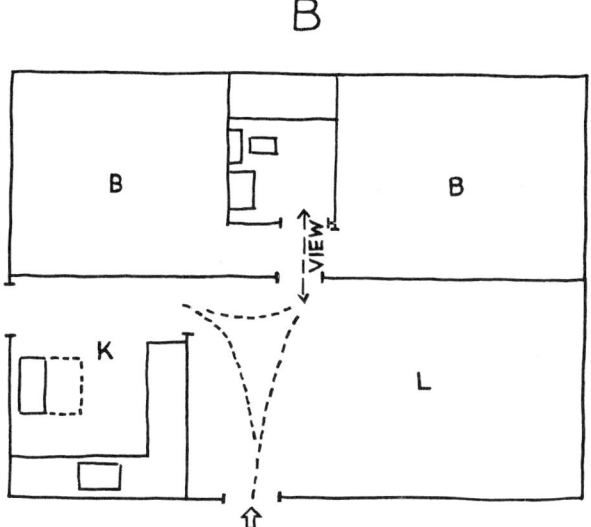

The addition of a small central hall has removed the faults of plan A. But you can see into the bath from the living room.

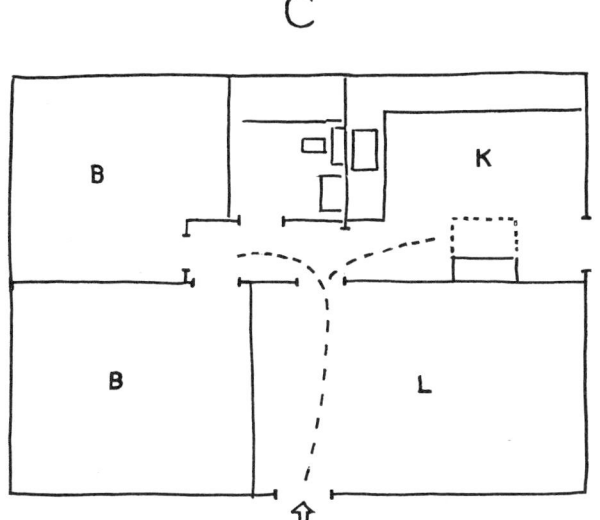

Placing the bedrooms at the end of the plan instead of across the back allows the plumbing to be concentrated.

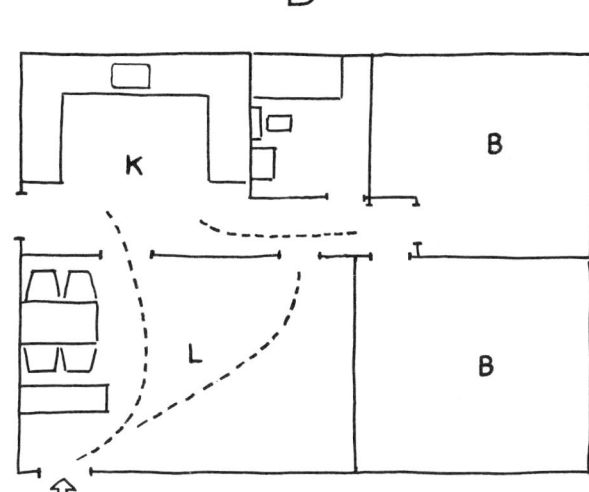

This entrance hall is hardly justified because it does not save traffic through the living room. Living space is cramped.

------- TRAFFIC LINES

Figure 2

Plans of minimum size.

Plan C offers a more economical grouping of plumbing, where bathroom fixtures and kitchen sink are back to back against the same wall. In plan D, the dining space has been partially marked off by a storage cabinet, which also forms a small entrance hall. Such an arrangement has some advantages, but the apparent size of the living room has been reduced by the division of space, and traffic lines cut across it in two directions.

EXERCISES

1. Make a collection of house plans, clipped from magazines, for use in later chapters.

2. Collect booklets and other information on prefabricated houses. Determine from local dealers what kinds of prefabricated houses are available in your town.

READING REFERENCES

Bruce, Alfred, and Harold Sandbank. A History of Prefabrication. John B. Pierce Foundation. New York. 1944.

Callender, John H. Before You Buy a House. Crown Publishers. New York. 1953.

Graff, Raymond, Rudolph Matern, and Henry Williams. The Prefabricated House. Doubleday & Company, Inc. Garden City, New York. 1947.

Johnstone, B. K., and others. Building or Buying a House. McGraw-Hill Book Company, Inc. New York. 1945.

Kelly, Burnham. The Prefabrication of Houses. Technical Press. Massachusetts Institute of Technology. Boston. 1951.

McKennee, O. W., and others. Prefabs on Parade. The Housing Institute, Inc. New York. 1948.

Meredith, L. Douglas. How to Buy a House. Harper & Brothers. New York. 1947.

Tucker, Milton. Buying an Honest House. Little Brown & Company. Boston. 1930.

MAGAZINES CONTAINING MATERIAL ON HOUSE DESIGN

Architectural Record
Arts and Architecture
House and Garden
House and Home
House Beautiful
Progressive Architecture

Chapter II
Planning to Build

"Architecture is my delight, and putting up and pulling down, one of my favorite amusements."
Thomas Jefferson

If you live in the country, or in a town too small to support a good commercial building enterprise, or if you would not be satisfied with a tract house, you can build on your own. The best way to do it is to employ an architect to plan the house and supervise the building. In this way you will obtain a house that is planned particularly to suit your own ideas, your way of life, and your family.

An owner-built house can have better design and more individuality than you find in the average commercially built house. The materials and methods of building will be of your own choice. You will, however, have to give your own time and effort in working with the architect, in order to get the best possible house for your investment.

For some people, building a house is so challenging and interesting that it is worth the effort. If you enjoy building, the satisfaction of sharing in a creative enterprise is compensation enough for the trouble you take.

The best way to prepare for building or buying a house is to make a study of plans. By observing real houses as well as plans on paper, you can develop the judgment you will need for making a wise choice of a plan. There are so many variations in the way space in a house can be arranged and divided that it takes practice to understand them, and to learn which one suits you best.

A plan is the quickest and most exact method of expressing your ideas on space arrangements within a house. A written description of the layout of rooms might be misinterpreted, because words are sometimes ambiguous. That is why plans, drawn to scale, are a part of the building contract.

A sense of space is immensely useful to the amateur house planner. Having a sense of space means being able to see with your mind's eye just how large a room or a piece of furniture is, as you look at the plan on paper. This feeling for space can only be acquired by your own efforts. Nobody can give it to you.

In order to acquire a sense of space you must form the habit of noticing the sizes of rooms and of furniture. Wherever you find yourself, try to guess the size of the room by studying it and comparing it with your memory of rooms that are familiar to you. Then verify your guess by finding out the actual size. After a few such efforts you will find that your guesses are becoming more accurate. If you memorize the appearance of a few objects of standard size, such as nine by twelve foot rugs, or a double or single bed, you will have a useful mental yardstick for estimating other sizes.

A collection of plans clipped from magazines makes a good starting point for studying houses. For your first exercise in judgment, choose a small one-story house that interests you. Since plans in magazines are usually too small to study easily, it will be worth your while to copy it in a larger scale. Making a copy is more useful than just looking at the plan, because it helps you think of it as a real house, rather than lines on paper.

The word "scale" mentioned above means the use of any given measure in a drawing to represent one foot in the actual house. The easiest way for the beginner to do a scale drawing is to use paper printed in 1/4-inch squares. Each of these squares will represent one square foot in the plan. It is a good thing to let your eye become accustomed to this scale of 1/4-inch to the foot, for it is commonly used in the blueprints when a house is built.

To start your copy of the plan, draw first the partition that makes the longest straight line through the house. Then add the various rooms on each side of it. The sizes of halls, closets, and bathrooms are not usually given, but they can be estimated by comparing them with some dimension that is stated. Figures 3, 4, 5, and 6 show some details of plans. These are simplified versions of the way architects draw them on blue-prints.

Doors open into rooms, swinging back out of the way as you enter. Draw them standing wide open, to make sure that they will not strike a piece of furniture. You may prefer to use one of the modern doors that fold or slide out of the way, for they allow better use of floor space. A common mistake of beginning house-planners is to skimp on the width of doors. A standard door is 2'8" wide, and a few extra inches must be allowed on each side for the frame. You can see then that a space 3' wide is barely enough to hang a door. Closet doors, however, may be of less than standard size.

A plan is not complete without at least the larger pieces of furniture. You can use little paper patterns cut to scale to represent the various pieces. Shift them about until you have the best arrangement; then draw a line around them for a permanent record.

Place the larger pieces of furniture first, where you think they will be most useful and convenient, as well as pleasant to look at. The sizes of the various wall spaces will govern their placing to some extent. A restful, orderly appearance is gained by placing the large pieces parallel to the wall, or, in some cases, at right angles to it. Some modern arrangements make use of diagonal lines in both walls and in furniture placing, but it takes an expert to do it well. If it is done badly, the room will have the disorganized, temporary look of housecleaning time. In a small room, leaving an open area in the middle of the floor creates an illusion of space.

The spaces between are just as important as the furniture itself. Leave plenty of room for yourself to move around and use the furniture. With a little experimenting you can determine how much space you need to walk easily between two pieces of furniture, to stretch out in an armchair without feeling that your legs are cramped, to stoop and pull out a drawer in a chest, to make a bed, and all the other activities involved in living in a house.

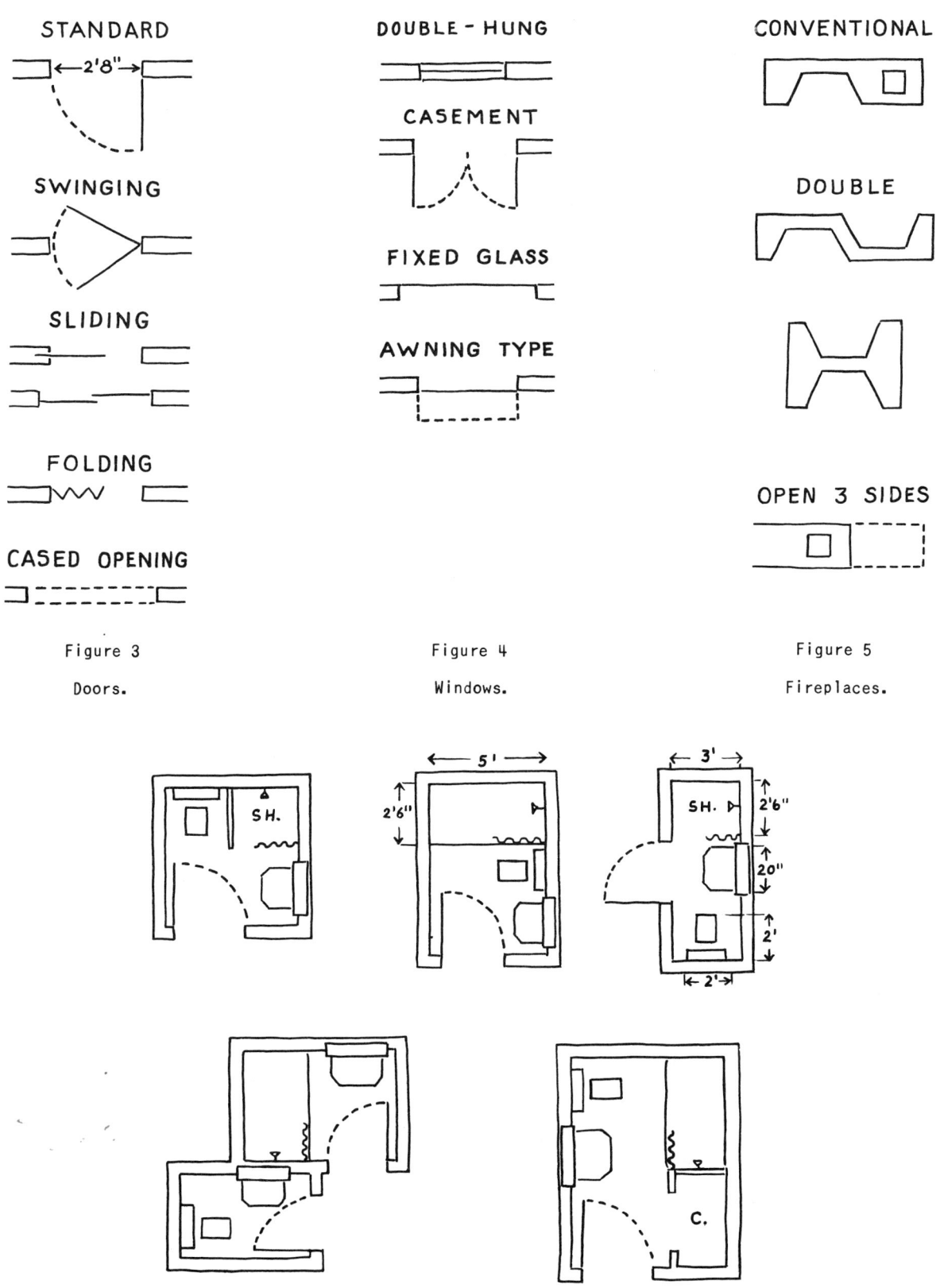

Figure 3 Doors.

Figure 4 Windows.

Figure 5 Fireplaces.

Figure 6 Bathrooms.

Sizes of furniture vary so much that it is not easy to boil them down to a simple list. The following table gives sizes ranging from the smallest to the largest that you would be likely to use in a house of average size.

	Width	Length
Armchair	2' - 3'	2' - 3'
Side chair	18" - 20"	18" - 20"
Sofa	2'6" - 3'	6' - 8'
Love seat	2'6" - 3'	4' - 5'
Desk		
Secretary	18" - 24"	3' - 4'
Kneehole	18" - 24"	3' - 5'
Piano		
Spinet	2'	5'
Baby grand	5'	5'
Dining table		
To seat 6	2'6" - 3'	4' - 5'
Sideboard	18" - 2'	4' - 6'
Double bed	4'6"	6'10"
Single bed	2'6" - 3'3"	6'10"
Studio couch	30"	6'
Dresser, chest, etc.	18" - 2'	3' - 5'

If the front door opens directly into the living room, a path to the rest of the house should be kept clear of furniture. All such lines of traffic may be marked with a dotted line. Then you will be reminded not to place furniture where it will be in the way. Figure 7 shows traffic lines in a small living room.

The practice of arranging chairs and sofa in a close huddle about the fireplace was reasonable in the old days, when the open fire was the sole source of heat, and the only warm area in a room was the section about the hearth. Today, the central heating unit warms the entire house, and open fires are used chiefly for their decorative and sentimental value. You need not sit close to the fire to be comfortable. It is more important that everyone in the room should be able to see the fire.

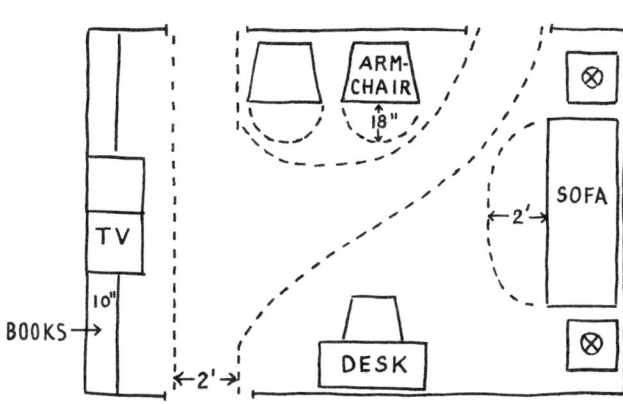

Figure 7

Traffic lanes in a living room.

The fireplace itself has broken away from its traditional position, and is not always set flat in the wall. Sometimes it is built into the end of a partial partition, where it may be enjoyed from three sides, as in Figure 8, or it is set out in the center of the floor, under a metal hood.

For the combination living-dining room the regulation dining table usually takes too much space. A drop-leaf table, or some other adjustable form is more useful. Some tables are adjustable in height as well as in size; between meals they may be lowered and made

Figure 8

A fireplace may be enjoyed from three sides.

smaller, to serve as coffee tables. Tall storage cabinets have been designed for double duty; they have a hinged front that drops down to form a table (Figure 9). Silver and linens may be stored in such a cabinet, or in a low chest of drawers, instead of the rather unwieldy sideboard of traditional design. The dining area may be partly separated from the rest of the room by placing a cabinet or other piece at right angles to the wall. It takes a fairly large room, however, to stand such division without looking crowded. Figure 10 shows a partial separation of the dining area.

A desk in the living room is intended for casual use by more than one member of the family, and constant vigilance is needed to keep it from becoming a catch-all for odd envelopes and tired

Figure 9

A combination storage cabinet and dining table.

rubber bands. A desk needs to be placed away from traffic lines through the room, and, if it is used for writing, it needs a good light from the left. If a desk is to be used for serious and prolonged work, it belongs in its owner's bedroom, unless there is an extra room to serve as study or office.

The piano problem has been reduced by the development of the small-sized spinet type. Even the new baby grand pianos are smaller than the old ones. Various factors complicate the placing of a piano. Sunlight will injure the finish; dampness and sudden temperature changes may affect the tone; a good light must fall on the keys and the music, not on the player's face. The piano is no longer standard equipment for living rooms; there is no reason for having one unless it is used.

Figure 10

The dining area may be partly separated from the living area.

The location of the radio and the television set depend on their importance in your life. If listening to music is your favorite way of spending leisure time, the radio-phonograph might have to be placed first, in order to obtain the best tone. It is amusing to look back on the early impact of television. At first, when there were only a few sets, their owners' living rooms were filled every evening by friends and neighbors. Predictions were made then that the living room of the future would be like a tiny theater, with little furniture beside a television set and rows of chairs. Now, only a few years later, the living room is back to normal; in many houses the television set has been moved into another room, and there are some people who actually sit and read books in their leisure time.

A balanced arrangement of furniture contributes to an orderly, quiet feeling in a room. Large pieces should be placed far enough apart so that they will not make one part of the room seem too heavy and crowded. A large piece may be balanced by a group of several smaller ones. Whether you use a formally balanced arrangement, with the two sides of the room exactly alike, or a more casual informal balance, is a matter of personal choice.

You need not feel that every wall space and every corner must be filled before a room can be considered furnished. If you value space for its own sake, and many people do, you will want to leave some areas empty. It is hard to achieve a serene, restful feeling in a room if you crowd it with too much furniture.

When you plan the dining space, whether it is a separate room or a part of the living room, draw the chairs as they must be placed when in use, that is, with the front edge of the chair-seat in line with the edge of the table. It is no use to draw them pushed far under the table, for you cannot sit in them when they are in that position.

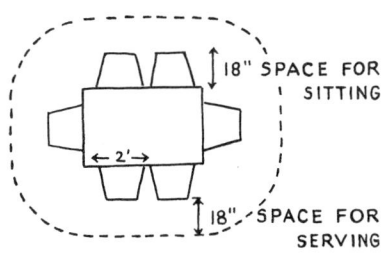

Figure 11

Spaces needed in a dining room.

Space requirements vary for dining. When a part of the living room is used, a little crowding, and some compromise in methods of serving may be unavoidable. A separate dining room in which meals are served with some degree of formality must be fairly spacious. Allow about two feet of table space for each diner, and at least 18" behind the chairs for serving. See Figure 11.

In the bedroom, you need space to move about in dressing, making the bed, putting your clothes away and running the vacuum cleaner. See Figure 12. The position of the bed may depend on the climate, at least until air-conditioning equipment becomes standard. Where nights are cool, ventilation is not much of a problem, but comfort in a hot climate depends on free circulation of air. Regardless of climate, avoid placing a double bed in a corner, if you can possibly find another place for it.

Chests and other storage furniture are placed after the best place has been found for the bed. Leave enough space in front of them so that you can stoop and pull out a lower drawer in comfort. Mirrors used in dressing are placed where the light falls on your face, rather than on the mirror itself.

In all other rooms follow the same procedure of placing the largest or most important pieces first, and then adding the smaller pieces where they will be most useful.

After you have placed the furniture, you are ready to judge the plan in terms of convenience and comfort in family living, appearance, and economy.

Convenient living is promoted by good circulation, which means ease in going from one part of the house to another. Extend the dotted line you have drawn from the front door to each bedroom, and to the kitchen. Add other lines to show the path from the kitchen to the dining area, from kitchen to bedrooms, and from bedrooms to the bath. Plans that have the shortest and simplest traffic lines may be considered to have the best circulation.

Good circulation calls for adequate hall space in relation to the size of the house. In an ideal plan, perhaps, no room would have to serve as a passageway. Economy, however, often forces us to compromise and use the living room or the dining room as a means of access to other rooms. No bedroom should be a passageway to another room.

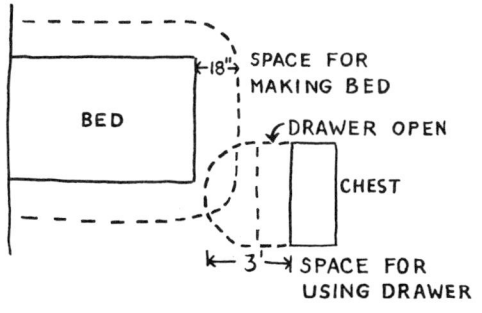

Figure 12

Spaces needed in a bedroom.

Perhaps no other single factor is so important to convenience as adequate storage space. When surveys are made of the faults of existing houses, lack of storage space heads the list. Minimum storage requirements call for a closet for each bedroom, and, in addition, a space for each of the following: coats, cleaning tools, linens, and seasonal storage, such as blankets and heavy coats through the summer months.

There have been many changes and improvements in household storage. As late as 50 years ago many houses were built with one or two large closets in which a great variety of things were kept. Modern storage is broken into smaller units, that are distributed about the house, so that our belongings may be kept in places convenient to their use.

Storage walls are a clever modern development that makes use of the space hitherto wasted between the studs of the old-fashioned partition. They are, in effect, ceiling-high storage cabinets that take the place of partitions. They may be from one to three feet thick, according to the things to be stored and the space that can be spared. Figure 13 shows a storage wall that serves as a partial partition between the kitchen and an all-purpose room.

Since the storage wall may include drawer space, shelves, desks, and bookcases, its cost is offset by the fact that there will be fewer pieces of furniture to buy. Storage walls may be purchased ready-made or they may be custom-built for a particular house. The use of movable storage cabinets as partitions suggests many possibilities in flexible planning to meet the changing needs of a growing family.

Other things that contribute to convenient and pleasant family life are enough comfortable chairs in the living room, a place for children to play and to store their toys, room for work and hobbies, and privacy, from the street, from the neighbors, and for individual members of the family.

The appearance of room interiors depends on the plan as well as on the furnishings and color scheme. The size and shape of rooms will give some indication of their possibilities in regard to beauty. A very small room will look crowded and uncomfortable with even the minimum amount of furniture; a room that is too narrow and very long is likely to resemble a corridor no matter how you arrange the furniture.

Figure 13

A storage wall serves as a partition.

Careless placing of windows and doors may break up the wall space so that the larger pieces of furniture will not fit. Windows of different width and height in the same room create a curtain problem. Rooms that are irregular in shape can be difficult to furnish. A quiet unbroken background will prove easy to live with over a period of years. Beauty in interiors is also enhanced by vistas from one room to another, and by pleasant views seen through the windows.

You might next study your plan in terms of economy. The cost of a house is related to its size, but the quality of materials and the workmanship are also important. We cannot make strict rules about how large a house may be. Spacious rooms are pleasant, if we can afford to build and to heat them. On the other hand, very small rooms can be wearing on the spirit, even if they are adequate to hold us and our furniture.

It is really questionable economy to make a house too small, because such expensive things as heating, plumbing, wiring, and kitchen equipment will cost about the same, whether we have rooms of comfortable size or pinch them down to little boxes. The extra cost of a few more square feet of floor space is relatively small in proportion to the total cost of the house.

Individual temperament is involved in our feelings about the size of rooms. Some people are happier with large rooms and high ceilings, while others feel more secure in small enclosures. Some people think of large rooms in terms of the amount of work required to keep them clean, or of the extra yards of carpeting, wallpaper, and curtaining to be paid for, or the extra fuel to keep warm in winter.

There are limits of size, however, below which a room may not fall, if it is to accommodate the usual furniture. The following table shows the approximate dimensions of rooms, compiled from a number of moderately priced houses built in recent years. The sizes needed for rooms depends to some extent on the type of plan. More space is needed when the rooms are definitely separated from one another; in the open plan, where living, dining, and kitchen space run together and partly overlap, the total floor space may be reduced.

Table of Room Sizes

	Width in feet	Length in feet
Living room	11 to 15	15 to 25
Dining room	10 to 15	12 to 16
Dining alcove	5 to 7	7 to 9
Kitchen	7 to 10	10 to 18
Utility room	6 to 8	8 to 10
Double bedroom	10 to 14	12 to 18
Single bedroom	8 to 10	10 to 15
Extra room Play, study, etc.	8 to 10	10 to 16
Bathroom	5 to 8	7 to 9
Lavatory	3 to 5	4 to 6
Entrance hall	4 to 6	5 to 8
Back hall	3 to 4	4 to 6
Stairway	3 to 3-1/2	10 to 15
Single car garage	9 to 10	18 to 22

The shape of the plan affects the cost. An extended, irregular house with broken roof lines will cost more than the same amount of floor space in a compact rectangle. Generally speaking, the closer a plan comes to a square shape, the more economical it is to build. An extended plan may be worth its extra cost, if you can afford it, because it provides a larger number of corner rooms with windows on two or even three sides.

The way space is used within the house is related to economy. Large halls and small rooms, for instance, represent a wasteful use of space. But, on the other hand, some hall space is needed, for it promotes easy circulation and allows greater privacy for individual members of the family.

Other types of hall space are related to the size and cost of the house, also. A separate entrance hall is a good thing, if you can afford it, for it keeps traffic out of the living room, saving wear on the rug and labor in keeping it clean. But, if you must economize, you may have to do without an entrance hall, and let the front door open directly into the living room. In very cold climates, even small houses need vestibules, even though they take up space; they pay for themselves by preventing loss of heat when the door is opened.

Grouping the rooms that contain plumbing fixtures in the same section of the house promotes economy. Such an arrangement is fairly easy in small one-story houses, but more difficult in the large, rambling houses that are popular today. The larger and more costly the house, presumably the less need there is for strict economy.

The amount of plumbing depends on the size and cost of the house. At the lowest price levels, one bathroom is all that can be expected. If you can afford to spend a few thousand dollars more, your house ought to have a lavatory or a second bathroom, especially if there are more than two bedrooms. If money is no object, it is reasonable to include a bathroom for each bedroom, as well as more lavish plumbing equipment in the kitchen and utility areas, such as a sink for flower arrangement.

The group of plans in Figure 14 a-b-c is in a slightly higher price range than those of Figure 2, even though they are still two-bedroom houses. They are a little larger, and contain dining areas apart from the living room.

In one respect these plans are superior to those of the preceding group. They recognize the outdoor living area behind the house, marked "O.L.", and provide access to it without going through the kitchen. In A and B, the traffic lines cover too much of the living room. In C, the living room at the back of the house is out of the main traffic lines, but you must cross the entrance hall to reach the bathroom from either one of the bedrooms. Interchanging the position of the entrance hall and the bath would correct this fault, but plumbing costs would be higher through this separation of the fixtures. F.H.A. loans have recently been approved for houses with inside bathrooms, if they have a proper ventilating fan. Figure 14 D shows a plan with such a bathroom.

PLANNING TO BUILD 17

Indoor and outdoor living areas are closely related in these plans.

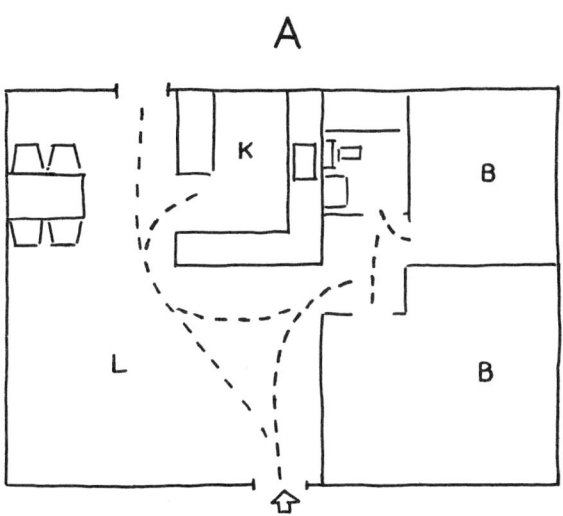

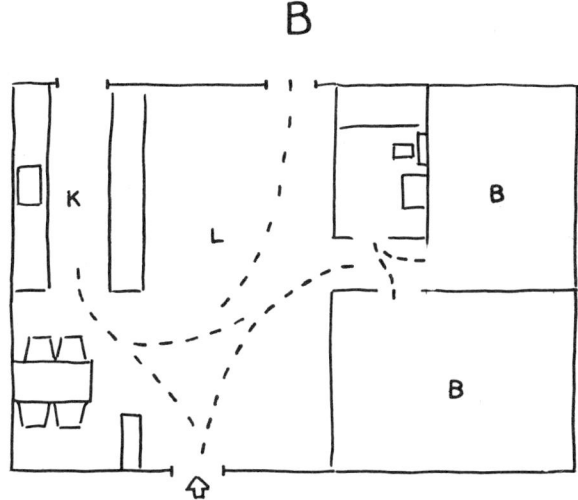

Concentrated plumbing, but much traffic in living room.

Far too much traffic in living room.

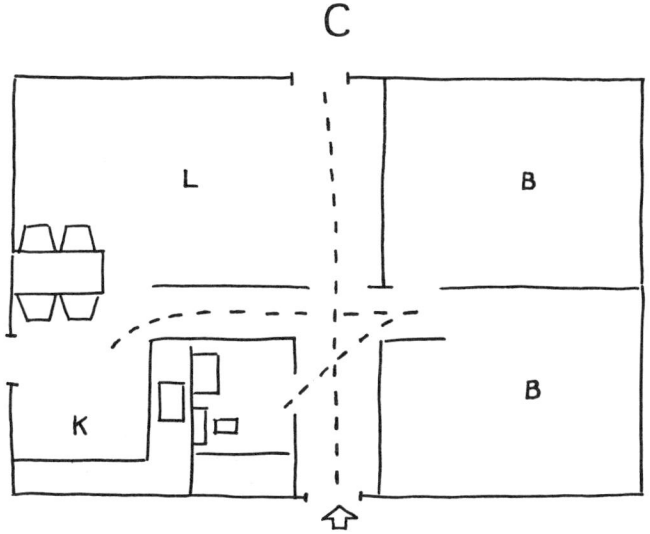

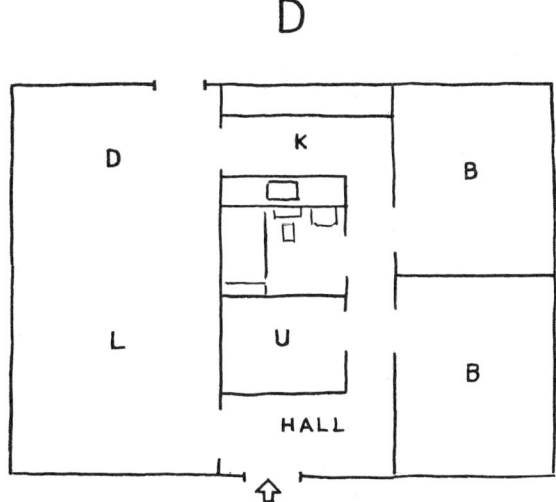

Separation of bedrooms from bath by entrance hall is too high a price to pay for grouped plumbing.

The utility-core plan allows maximum use of outside walls for important rooms.

Figure 14

Two-bedroom plans.

EXERCISES

1. Since the cost of building varies in different parts of the country, specific figures would not be useful here. The approximate cost of the plan you are studying may be estimated by comparing it with similar houses in your locality. Study the prices in real estate advertisements in your newspaper. You can also get a rough estimate of the cost of a house by computing its area and multiplying it by the current cost per square foot of building in your community.

2. Select one of the plans of Figure 14, and draw it to scale. You will have to decide on the exact sizes of the rooms, using your best judgment. Place the furniture, and list the good and bad features of the plan.

READING REFERENCES

Allen, Paul. *Build Your Own Adobe*. Stanford University Press. Palo Alto, Calif. 1946.

Corey, Paul. *Build a Home*. Dial Press. New York. 1946.

Ford, James, and Katherine Morrow Ford. *Design of Modern Interiors*. Architectural Book Publishing Company, Inc. New York. 1942.

Graf, Jean, and Don Graf. *Practical Houses for Contemporary Living*. F. W. Dodge Corporation. New York. 1953.

Hennessey, William J., Ed. *America's Best Small Houses*. The Viking Press. New York. 1949.

Laidman, Hugh. *How to Build Your Own House*. Harper & Brothers. New York. 1950.

Mock, Elizabeth. *If You Want to Build a House*. Simon & Schuster, Inc. New York. 1946.

Nelson, George, and Henry Wright. *Tomorrow's House*. Simon & Schuster, Inc. New York. 1945.

Reid, Marshall, Ed. *When You Build*. Robert M. McBride & Company. New York. 1946.

Chapter III
Drawing the Exterior

*"When we mean to build
We first survey the plot,
Then draw the model;"*
  Shakespeare: Henry IV

The outside appearance of a house may be shown by elevations, that is, flat diagrams of the outside walls. Since elevations represent height and width but not depth, they need to be studied with the plan to give a complete picture of the house. Elevations, like plans, may be drawn to scale, to show the exact size of every detail. For that reason they serve as part of the building contract.

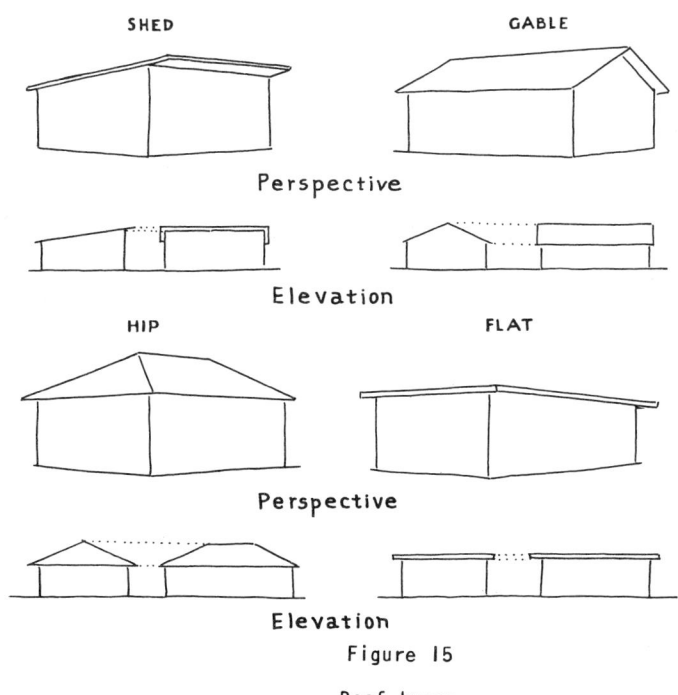

Figure 15

Roof types.

Before you begin to draw the elevations for one of the plans you have studied, look at pictures of small houses as found in books and current magazines, and select a few of them to guide you in your drawing. Houses that have been designed by qualified architects provide the best guide, because their designs are the outcome of special training. Note the size, type, and arrangement of windows and doors, and any details of their setting. Figure 15 shows a number of the roof types in use today, and windows are shown in Figure 16. In modern design, window frames are usually kept simple and unobtrusive.

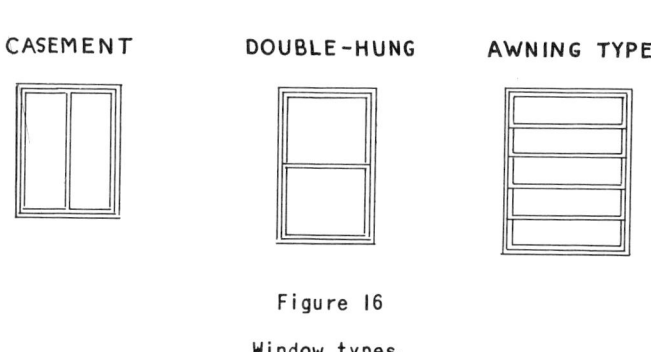

Figure 16

Window types.

The elevations of your house may be drawn on the same squared paper you used for the plan, or they may be drawn on plain paper, with the help of a T-square and triangle. You can make a scale ruler by marking the edge of a strip of stiff paper to match the squares on the paper used for the plan.

Draw the narrow side of the house (the left-hand view in figure 17) first, in order to determine the slant of the roof. Note that the roof is indicated by a horizontal line in the long, or right-hand view.

An elevation is drawn from the ground up, just as a house is built. First draw a freehand horizontal line in the lower part of your paper, to represent the ground level, then set up vertical lines for the walls, and draw the roof over it. Figure 17 shows how the plan is related to the exterior elevations. When a real house is built, all four elevations are drawn, but two sides may be enough to express your ideas.

Figure 17

Relation of plan to elevation.

The floor and ceiling levels may be shown by light dotted lines. The height of the foundation varies from a few inches for a slab house, to a foot or more for houses with basements. Low foundations are generally preferred because they contribute to a solid, substantial appearance, and make the house look as if it belongs to the site.

Ceiling heights for small houses are about 8 feet, but they vary with the size and type of house, and the climate. In hot countries high ceilings are needed for comfort, while low ones save fuel where winters are severe. Economy in the use of standard lumber sizes is also a factor in determining the height of the ceiling.

Use your own judgment about the height of the ridgepole. Sketch in lightly several roof lines at different angles, and choose the one you think best. When the end elevation has been outlined, and before any windows are placed, draw one of the long sides of the house.

Draw the windows in lightly at first, according to their position on the plan. If this arrangement is not pleasing in appearance, you may have to change the plan a bit, so that the exterior design will be better. Windows and doors are bought ready-made in standard sizes. Decide first on the sizes that look best in relation to the design of the house, for stock sizes may be found within a few inches of them. You will also have to keep an eye on the arrangement of furniture, so that it does not conflict with the windows.

The height of doors and windows, like many other measurements in a house, are related to human sizes. Doors need to be high enough so that a tall man may walk through easily. They must be wide enough so that parcels and furniture may be carried easily, and also so that we may walk through without any danger of knocking our hands against the sides of the frame.

Since even a small house may have windows of several different sizes, you will have to determine their size according to their use. In general, windows should extend up near to the ceiling, because the best light comes in through the upper part. If the windows are set too low in the wall, the room will be dark except when the sun shines directly in. It is pleasant, also, to be able to look out at the sky whether you are standing or sitting down. This means that the top of a window must be higher than a tall man's eyelevel.

It is not true that doors and windows should always maintain the same level at their tops. Doors and windows differ so widely in their functions that they cannot be governed by the same rules. Where the ceilings are high, windows will naturally be taller than doors, for light and air are better distributed through the room if the windows extend up close to the ceiling. On the other hand, a height of about 7 feet is enough for doors, and there is no reason for making them taller. If you study pictures of Colonial mansions with high-ceilinged rooms, you will see that the windows are considerably higher than the doors.

The height of window sills is governed often by the room. Above a kitchen sink or counter they must be from 3 to 4 feet above the floor. In other rooms, if you want to see out when you are sitting down, they cannot be much more than 2 feet high. Usually lower sills are used in living and dining rooms, and somewhat higher ones in bedrooms and bath. The so-called "shoulder-high" windows, that is, small windows placed high in the wall, are used today in some houses. Such windows are cheap, and they allow the placing of standard furniture in the tiny bedrooms so often found in low-cost tract houses. Their disadvantages are that you cannot see out, and on hot nights the circulation of air is too far above the level of the bed to keep you cool. Anyone who has lived in a house of the bungalow era, the last time "shoulder-high" windows were used, knows that they leave much to be desired. In addition to limiting light and air, they present a curtaining problem, and give a room a closed-in feeling.

Figure 18

High windows allow freedom in furniture arrangement, but are inadequate for light and air.

Before you decide on the type and placing of the windows, read Chapter XIII. Balance is achieved by arranging the windows so that neither side of the facade is too heavy for the other. Order and unity result from the use of the same or similar kinds of window, or, if they are unlike in size, using a uniform division of spaces. It is hard to use both double-hung and casement windows together, for the former have a horizontal division, and the latter a vertical division.

Study pictures of doorways for ideas on drawing your own. Note especially the kind of doors used by architects, as compared with those found in tract houses. The door with three little windows set diagonally is looked on with disfavor by architects, not so much because it is a sort of trademark of the tract house, but because it is not good in design. The diagonal line created by the three windows is not related to the structural lines of the door, and destroys its unity and order.

After the drawing is made, use colored pencils or water color to indicate the materials of wall and roof, the ground beneath the house, and a few shrubs.

Chapter IV
Planning the Kitchen

"Home is the girl's prison and the woman's workhouse."
George Bernard Shaw

The kitchen deserves special consideration because a large share of the work of housekeeping is done in it and a great deal of money is spent on its equipment. The arrangement of the kitchen is based on an orderly progress of work in preparing meals and cleaning up. The main work centers are the sink, the range, and the preparation counter. Storage space is provided for utensils and supplies at the center where they are first used.

The term "center" must not be interpreted to mean detached units. They are connected by a continuous counter or working surface. No other kitchen furniture, such as a planning desk, or the breakfast table, should be allowed to break into this counter.

The key to good kitchen arrangement is the proper placing of doors. Their number should be kept to the minimum, and as far as possible, they should be grouped together in order to allow long unbroken wall spaces. Closet doors opening into a kitchen are open to question, because they take wall space that should be used for equipment or counters. If the back door opens into the kitchen, it should be placed so that the traffic line will not run through the working area of the kitchen.

Because the sink is used in connection with practically all kitchen operations, a central position between the range and the refrigerator makes it easily reached from all parts of the working surface. A sink should never be placed in a corner, where only one person can approach it at a time. Counter spaces or drainboards on both sides of a sink are so useful that they should always be provided. Storage space at the sink takes care of all supplies and utensils used in such food preparation as washing and cutting vegetables, and in dishwashing.

Some women like to have the sink under a window; others dislike facing the light and the risk of chipping the dishes, when their attention is drawn outdoors. Double sinks, or a combination of sink and dishwasher, are considered standard equipment for new houses.

The depth of kitchen equipment has been standardized at about two feet. The table below shows the width of various pieces used in the kitchen.

Single sink	24" to 30"
Double sink	32"
Range	22" to 40"
Refrigerator	24" to 36"
Dish washer	24"
Washing machine	24" to 30"
Clothes dryer	24" to 30"
Ironer	30" to 40"

A section of the counter space is set apart for a preparation center, with storage space above and below for mixing bowls, baking pans, flour, and other staples. The electric mixer is stationed on or next to this counter. Even if you use ready-made mixes, you will still need ample space at this counter for rolling out pastry or setting out cookie sheets and cake pans. Two useful kitchen arrangements are shown in Figure 19.

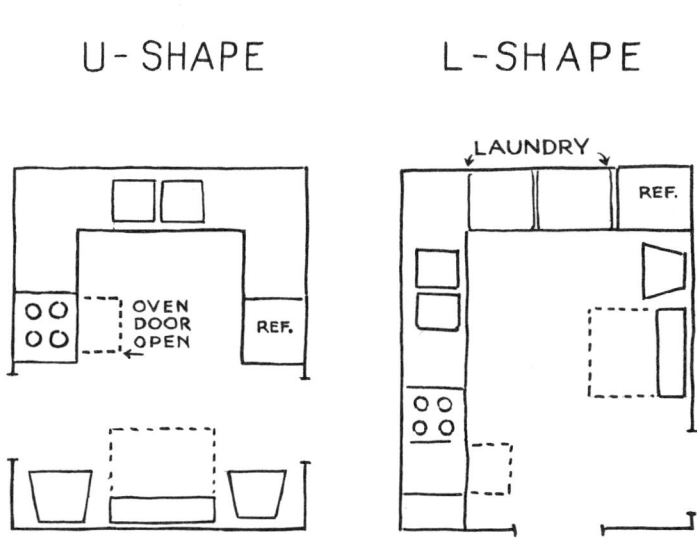

Figure 19

Standard kitchen arrangements.

The dishing up of hot foods from the range to the table needs to be done quickly. A serving counter next to the range provides a place for assembling plates and serving dishes, both on their way to the table and on their return journey after the meal. The serving counter may also be used as an auxiliary to the range during baking and other cooking operations.

At the cooking center, storage space is needed for those cooking pans whose use begins at the range, and for lids, pot holders, stirring spoons, and meat forks. A tall narrow cupboard with hooks set in its sides makes a convenient place for hanging pans and skillets; lids and shallow pans may be kept in wire racks on the inside of a cupboard door on a shelf with narrow vertical divisions. A little shelf space above the range should be provided for seasonings that are added during cooking.

An interesting development in range design is the separation of the oven and the broiler from the surface cooking units. One advantage of such separation is that the heat from the oven or broiler will be kept away as you work over the service units. If you do not like to stoop, the oven may be set up on top of the counter or it may be set into the wall.

The refrigerator is a highly specialized part of the kitchen storage space. The only work done directly at it consists of arranging and cleaning. A counter space next to the refrigerator makes such work easier. If a separate counter cannot be included, the mixing counter may double as an auxiliary to the refrigerator, because you will not be cleaning it at the same time that you are baking. The proper place for a refrigerator is at the end of the counter. On no account should it be placed where it breaks up the counter between two work centers, such as the sink and range.

The height of working surfaces in a kitchen presents a problem that is still to be solved. No one has figured out how to make kitchen equipment adjustable in height. The standard height of 3 feet, commonly used for ranges and counters, is a bit too low for very tall women, and too high for short ones. If you expect to live permanently in your house, you can have the height that suits you best. Since it is only sensible to do as much work as possible sitting down, at least one lower surface should be provided, with knee space below.

Abundant shelf space for utensils and dishes does away with the need for crowding or stacking them. The result is greater convenience in use, as well as fewer chipped edges. If all the wall spaces above equipment and counters are filled in with cupboards, enough storage space will be provided for the average family. It has been common practice to drop the ceiling down about twelve inches above the wall cabinets, to eliminate the dangers incidental to climbing on a chair to reach the top shelf. If you do not like the idea of wasting that space, you can extend the cupboards to their full height, and use the top shelf for extra supplies, and for utensils that are seldom used.

It used to be the fashion to say that the kitchen should be a sanitary workshop, dedicated to the preparation of food, and small enough so that cooking and clearing away could be done with only a step or two in any direction, but such theories did not stand up in actual practice. The hours spent in the kitchen are woven into the complex and varied fabric of the homemaker's life. They are not like the time spent by the factory worker at a machine. The purpose of efficient kitchen arrangement is not so much to enable the homemaker to turn out work with machine-like speed, as to make kitchen activities a pleasant and satisfying part of family living.

In recent years the trend has been toward larger kitchens. The passing of the separate dining room and of the basement have contributed to this trend. When there is no dining room the tendency is to eat many of the family meals in the kitchen. As a result the kitchen has had to grow larger to accommodate tables and chairs. Play space for small children, a mending corner, and a worktable for hobbies are among the other things that are finding their way back into the kitchen. In many ways the modern kitchen resembles the kitchen of the old-fashioned farmhouse of pioneer days. Figure 20 shows the plan of what is sometimes called a "country kitchen."

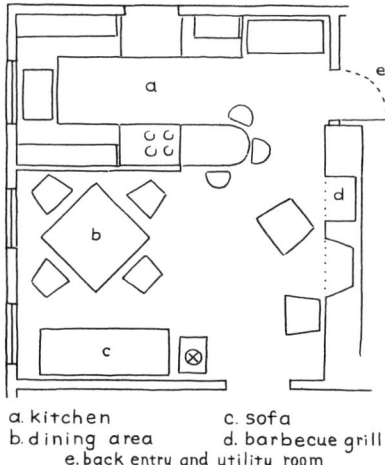

a. kitchen   c. sofa
b. dining area   d. barbecue grill
e. back entry and utility room

Figure 20

A kitchen combined with an all-purpose room.

When there is no basement in the house, utility space for the heating unit, the water heater, and for laundry equipment is needed on the first floor, next to, and sometimes merged into, the kitchen area. The newest laundry equipment is so compact that it can be absorbed into the kitchen without too much trouble, but some women do not like to do the laundry in the kitchen because of the steam and heat involved.

Automatic washing and drying machines have changed our laundry habits. The weekly washday, when all other household activities are suspended, is no longer necessary. Many women find it convenient to do several small washings a week; others keep ahead of their laundry problem by running one load through the washer each day. There is also much less ironing to be done today, because of our more informal way of dressing and also through the use of materials for clothing and household use that require little or no ironing.

EXERCISES

1. Make a collection of clippings from current magazines showing various types of kitchen equipment, as well as booklets and other literature offered by manufacturers.

2. Draw a plan to scale of the kitchen in your own home. Using tracing paper over the original drawing, try out several new arrangements that would promote greater efficiency.

3. Draw the kitchen of one of the plans in Figure 14 to scale, showing equipment and storage space in detail.

READING REFERENCES

Hawkins, Reginald R. The Kitchen Book. D. VanNostrand Company, Inc. New York. 1953.

Peet, Louise, and Lenore Thye. Household Equipment. Chap. 12. John Wiley & Sons, Inc. New York. 1950.

Rogers, Tyler S. Plan Your House to Suit Yourself. Charles Scribner's Sons. New York. 1950.

Shank, Naomi. Make Your Kitchen Modern. Agricultural Extension Bulletin, P 92. Iowa State College, Ames, Iowa. 1948.

Sooy, Louise, and Virginia Woodbridge. Plan Your Own Home. Stanford University Press. California. 1950.

University of Illinois. Handbook of Kitchen Design. Urbana, Ill. 1950.

Chapter V
A House Should Fit the Family

"The best security for civilization is the dwelling, and upon proper and becoming dwellings depends more than anything else the improvement of mankind."

Benjamin Disraeli

The earlier chapters dealt with the rather simple problems of judging very small houses. When you study larger plans, judging becomes more complicated. The larger and more costly the house, the more you should expect of it, in three respects: first, it should meet the needs and preferences of the family that will live in it; second, it should fit the site, and take full advantage of the contour of the land, and of the view; third, it should suit the climate in its plan, materials, and equipment.

The first requirement that any house must meet in regard to the family concerns the sleeping accommodations. It is not by accident that real estate dealers speak of houses in terms of the number of bedrooms they contain. Except for very large, costly houses, the living, dining, and cooking facilities remain fairly constant. We might say that a plan begins with the number of bedrooms needed. Minimum standards require a room for parents, and separate rooms for boys and for girls.

A number of factors enter into the problem of deciding between single and double bedrooms. Light sleepers may need bedrooms of their own. A combination bedroom and study may have to be provided for anyone who has work to do at home, and such a room cannot easily be shared. Two brothers or two sisters may be so far apart in age or in temperament that sharing a room becomes a hardship for one or both.

Some parents feel that a separate room for each child, no matter how small that room may be, promotes a smoothly-running household. Another argument for separate bedrooms grows from the present trend toward open plans; when the living, dining, and kitchen areas are thrown together, a bedroom provides the only chance for each member of the family to be alone. Privacy for individuals helps to combat the nervous strains of modern life.

When more than two bedrooms are needed, the plan as a whole is affected. Extra storage space must be added. The hall must be extended to open into each bedroom. A larger family needs more kitchen, dining, and living space. A separate entrance hall and additional bathroom facilities, while they might be considered luxuries, will make life easier for everyone.

These problems are not too difficult in a two-story house, but when they must be worked into a one-story plan, some compromises may be needed. For instance, cross-ventilation for all the bedrooms calls for a plan so irregular and extended that it may be too expensive. Judging by many of the houses built in recent years, home owners seem to like one-story houses so well that they are willing to put up with one or two quite small bedrooms that are without cross-ventilation.

In addition to the size of the family, the occupations, tastes, and ages of the various members may influence the plan. Studying your way of life and your interests, as every prospective home-owner should, may lead to some difficult decisions. You probably cannot afford everything that you would like to have in your house. You must choose the things you want most, and the other things that you are willing to forego in order to have them. A house is primarily a setting for happy, useful, family living, but the type of family and their ideas of happiness may have a bearing on the kind of house that will suit them best.

A family whose leisure-time interests lie mainly outside their home, who prefer sports or travel to staying home, would naturally have less money to spend on their living quarters, and might have to get along with a small, inexpensive house. Another family might enjoy spending their leisure time at home, engaged in various hobbies, or entertaining their friends. The money they save on outside diversions could be used to make their house larger and better equipped for their activities.

Your memories of pleasant experiences shared by your family will give you the clues to some of the ways in which the house can contribute to your own ideas of happy living. Entertaining friends, and quiet evenings at home, for instance, are enhanced by enough comfortable chairs, and good lighting for everyone, with tables and floor space for games and hobbies.

Other things that contribute to easier living within the family are enough storage space so that each member's possessions may be kept separate, and enough bathroom facilities to cope with the morning rush to get dressed and off to school or work. If the budget allows only one bathroom, the answer may be found in placing the fixtures in separate compartments. An arrangement of the plan that allows the living room to be kept reasonably neat for unexpected callers is another help in family living.

Daily meals are among the few occasions when many busy modern families are all together. Any event that occurs two or three times a day, and involves the entire family, certainly deserves to be made enjoyable. Unfortunately, mealtime arrangements have suffered as high building costs have squeezed the dining room out of the small house. Cramped little alcoves, where both ventilation and elbow room are lacking, and where members of the family must climb over one another to get in or out, are not conducive to pleasant mealtimes. Some parents feel that eating at a counter instead of sitting down to a properly set table, makes it more difficult to teach children proper eating habits and table manners. Comfortable seating, enough room for easy serving, and a pleasant view from the window, are not too much to ask for the dining area, whether it is in a separate room, or is a part of the living room, or of the kitchen.

Summertime meals out of doors are another source of happy memories of family life. While a fireplace at the far end of the garden may make such meals more like a picnic for the children, it entails much carrying back and forth, and often walking through wet grass. If the outdoor fireplace is built on a paved terrace next to the house, as in Figure 21, it will be so much easier to use that it will probably be used more often. A fireplace on the terrace also makes it possible to sit out of doors in quite cool weather.

Figure 21

An outdoor fireplace on the terrace.

Children need a place to play indoors in bad weather. If the rougher, more untidy kinds of play can be provided for outside of the living room, there will be less work in picking up and cleaning, not to mention less wear on the furniture, and unexpected callers are more likely to be greeted by an unflurried hostess.

The dining space that is usually included in or next to the kitchen in today's houses may be used for play, especially when children are small and need supervision from the kitchen. A folding table and lightweight chairs are more adaptable for child play than a permanently built-in dining alcove. If the back door is nearby older children may go from indoor to outdoor play areas without running through the living room. Other features that enhance the value of this space for children's play are a lavatory near the back entrance, and storage space for toys and wraps.

The three-bedroom plans in Figure 22-a-b-c naturally cover a larger area than do those in the preceding examples. Plans A and B are more economical than C, because of their compact rectangular shape. B has somewhat better circulation than A. Plan B, however, has one glaring fault. The carport covers all the windows of one of the bedrooms. Such a room would not even have daylight, not to mention sunshine, and exhaust fumes would constitute a health hazard. This is the type of fault you must be on guard against if you buy a tract house.

A HOUSE SHOULD FIT THE FAMILY

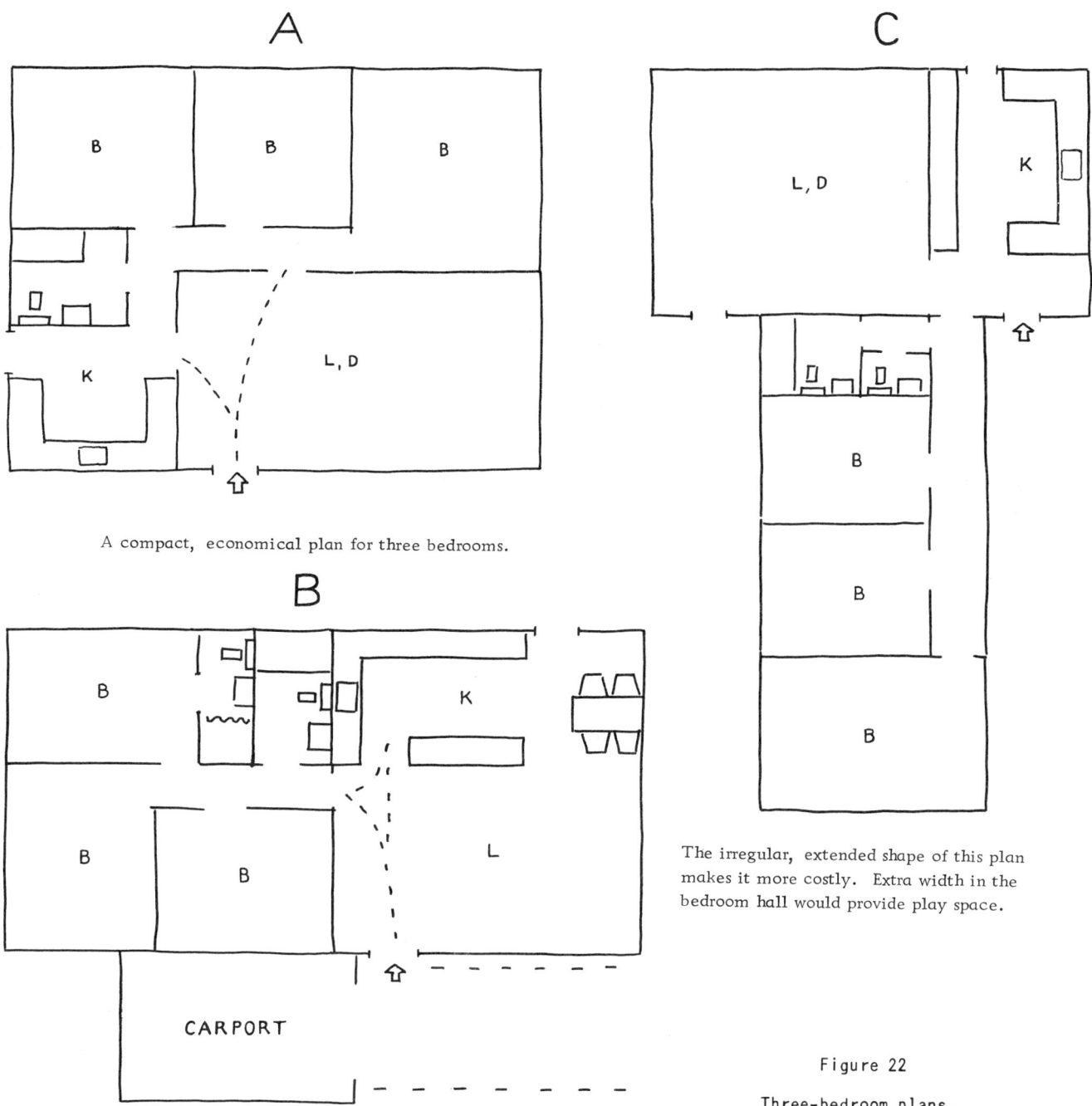

A compact, economical plan for three bedrooms.

A good plan completely spoiled by the position of the carport.

The irregular, extended shape of this plan makes it more costly. Extra width in the bedroom hall would provide play space.

Figure 22

Three-bedroom plans.

Many of the frictions of family life could be eased by a little extra space. Before high building costs forced the shrinkage of the middle-class house, there always used to be some sort of extra room. The victorian house had a back parlor or an upstairs sitting room, and its large attic provided play space for children as well as storage. More recently, houses had a recreation room in the basement, or a study on the first floor, or at least a separate dining room that could serve for other uses between meals. In late years, however, many houses have been built without basements, attics or dining rooms. They are scarcely adequate for any but the smallest families. An extra room, if you can afford it, can make life easier for everyone. If you buy a tract house, you might choose one with one more bedroom than you need for sleeping accommodations.

In a custom-built house, an extra room can be planned to meet your special needs. Its location depends to some extent on the use that is to be made of it, but generally it is best to have it accessible from more than one part of the house. The old-fashioned "sun parlor" was not fully useful as an extra room because it could be reached only by going through the living room.

If the extra room is placed where it may be used for several purposes, or converted later into another bedroom, it will enhance the resale value of the house. When the room is to be used for work or hobbies that create clutter, a location away from, or at least not visible from, the living room is indicated. It might be an extension of the kitchen or the utility room, or a connecting room between house and garage.

In some new houses you can see a return to the idea of the front and back parlors; that is, the living room is fairly small, and is reserved for quiet and relatively neat uses. Next to it is a room somewhat like the old-fashioned back parlor, that is used for informal living, work, hobbies, and child play. These two rooms may be separated by folding walls or movable storage cabinets instead of a permanent partition. Such an arrangement is useful for families that enjoy a lively social life, for the two rooms may be thrown together for large-scale entertaining. With the partition back in place, the second room will save the parents from having to sit in the kitchen when their daughters have dates.

Some houses make use of hall space for gaining an extra room. If any hall, other than the entrance, touches an outside wall so that it can have a window, it may be widened a bit to make it useful for child play, work, or informal meals, in addition to its use as a passageway. Plan C in Figure 22 has such a hall. If it were a few feet wider it could be used as a play-room. Here again we are reminded of an older type of plan. The large central hallway of the Georgian colonial house was furnished with sofa, chairs, and tables, and was used as an extension of the parlors.

The arrangements of space in Figure 23-a-b-c include an extra room, marked E, in addition to three bedrooms. In A, the extra room could be used in connection with the living room, for entertaining large groups of people. In B, the extra room has a more secluded position, and could be used for untidy activities that you would want to keep away from the living room. In either case, the extra room could be converted into a fourth bedroom.

C is another example of a utility-core plan, with an inside bathroom.

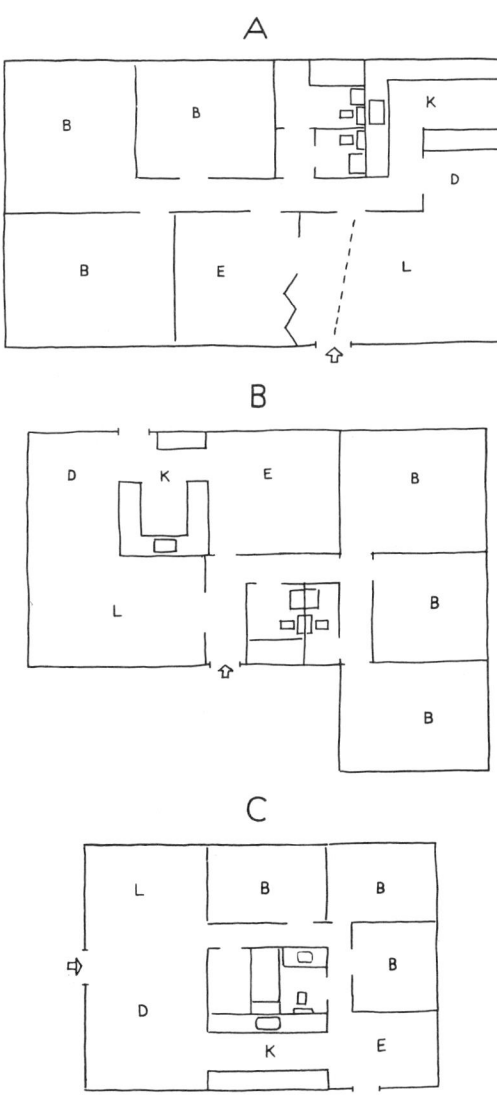

Figure 23

Plans with an extra room.

Planning a house to fit the family is complicated by the fact that the family itself changes, and the different stages in its development make varied demands on the dwelling. At first, a small house is sufficient, and is probably all a young family can afford. Somewhat larger quarters, and outdoor play space, are needed while the children are small. A third stage in the life of a family extends through the period when the children are attending the local schools. At this time the greatest amount of space is needed to provide for the children's activities and their expanding social life. The fourth stage sets in when the children begin to leave home to work, study, or marry. During this last stage the size and needs of the family diminish, until the parents are again alone. From then on there will be only occasional heavy demands on the house, when the children come home to visit.

These changing needs do not always apply to the same house. Many families have to move because of modern industrial conditions. When the breadwinner works for a large corporation, promotion often means moving to another part of the country. Jobs become scarce in one region and more plentiful in another. The widespread use of house trailers is evidence of the need for motility in a part of the population.

Even when a family lives all its life in the same city, moving may be the best answer to changing needs. Neighborhoods can deteriorate as the city grows. If you prosper, you will probably want to move to a less crowded, quieter section. The general trend in American living today is out of the cities into the suburban areas.

If you expect to live permanently in one house, you might built it a section at a time, adding space as it is needed, and as you can afford it. The plan of any house, of course, begins with the site, and in the case of an expanding house the probable future of the neighborhood is of more than ordinary importance. Choose a lot and a neighborhood that will be equal to the larger, more costly house that you expect to have in later years. It is difficult, if not impossible, to add extra rooms to a small house in a crowded development, not only because of the small size of the lot, but also because the character of the neighborhood does not justify a costly house. Country locations and roomy suburban lots make the best sites for houses that are destined to grow.

High building costs have led many young people to do their own construction as far as possible. The first unit may be as little as one room, kitchen, and bath, additional rooms being added during weekends and vacations. Power tools designed for the home workshop expedite the work of the amateur builder.

In a way, an expanding house should be planned backward, that is, it should be completed on paper in its final, largest stage, before the first part is built. It needs to be the type of plan that falls naturally into several sections, one of which can serve as the complete dwelling for the first stage of the family's life.

If the entire house is planned beforehand, additional space can be built on with a minimum of tearing out and rebuilding. Framing for future doors can be built into the walls from the start, and connections for future plumbing fixtures can also be installed. Movable storage walls may be used for temporary partitions. Enlarging a house is usually thought of in terms of adding bedrooms, but in some cases the bedroom section might be built first, one of them serving as a temporary living room until the second section is added.

Adding rooms to a house often calls for an extra hall. That hall must be planned with the first section of the house, or it may spoil one of the older rooms. It can be used as storage space until it is needed as a hall.

A final phase of the changing house might be its division. When the maximum space is no longer needed, the extra rooms may be converted into an apartment for rental, or for another change that often occurs in family life. If a grandparent or other elderly relative comes to live with the family, a self-contained apartment will afford some measure of privacy between the older and younger generations.

EXERCISES

1. The following list suggests some of the questions that might be asked as you study a plan in terms of family life. Add to it any other points that you consider important.

    a. Sleeping needs

        Are bedrooms protected from street noises and noise originating within the house?

        Are individual beds or rooms provided for those who need them?

        Are bedrooms shared by two people large enough; does an older person share a room with a child?

Is any bedroom used by the family as a short cut through the house?

Is storage space provided for each bedroom?

b. Dressing

Can each person's clothing be stored separately?

Is the bathroom convenient to all bedrooms without crossing the living area?

Is the bath adequate when all the family is dressing at the same time?

Are there enough well-lighted mirrors for shaving, hair combing, make-up, etc?

c. Cooking and eating

Can two people work in the kitchen without interfering with each other? Features that cause trouble are a sink or a stove in a corner, doors that open the wrong way, inadequate counter space.

Can any member of the family approach or leave the table without disturbing the others, or does a telephone call at mealtime cause a general upheaval?

d. Cleaning and laundry

Can tools for everyday, routine cleaning be taken out, used, and put away easily?

In a large house, is there an auxiliary cleaning closet up stairs or in the bedroom wing?

Does running the vacuum cleaner mean excessive moving of furniture?

Is the laundry close to the outdoor drying area, and is there a place indoors, other than the bathroom, for hanging up the daily handwashing of stockings, etc.?

Is the ironing equipment out of the way of traffic, apart from the working area of the kitchen, convenient for quick pressing jobs?

e. Children's needs

Can play areas for young children, both indoors and out, be seen from the kitchen?

Can they be used together without running through the living room?

Is there a place, other than the living room, for the rougher, more untidy kinds of play?

Is storage space for indoor toys convenient to the play area, and is there a place to keep larger outdoor things, such as tricycles?

Is there a well-lighted table for older children's study and hobbies, with storage for books, collections, and tools?

Can the older children entertain their friends without disrupting the life of the rest of the family?

Can each child find a place to be alone?

f. Adult needs

Can guests be welcomed at the front door, relieved of their wraps, and seated in the living room, without awkwardness?

Does adult entertaining involve rearranging the furniture and upsetting the family's normal life?

Do unexpected visitors cause a flurry of straightening and picking up?

Is there space for adult activities, such as hobbies and work that must be done at home, farm records, for instance?

2. Appraise your own home in terms of your family's needs, listing the ways in which it is adequate, and also how it might be improved.

3. List the special needs of a family of your acquaintance, or use one of the families described below, and select a plan that meets their requirements. Since imaginary situations are likely to become unrealistic, assume financial conditions similar to those of your own family. Planning for an unfamiliar social or economic environment can come too close to daydreaming. For the same reason, select a suitable locality, in either town or country, that is familiar to you.

4. a. Parents and three boys, 9, 11, and 14, one girl, 16. Father and boys enjoy sports, want ponies and dogs. Mother active in clubs, enjoys music.

b. Parents and three daughters, 12, 15, and 17. Grandmother spends several months of each year with family. Older girls are active socially, intend to go away to college; youngest shows ability as pianist, wants a career in music. Parents enjoy cards, travel.

c. Parents and two boys, 8 and 14, and one girl, 12. Father owns local business, mother works with him mornings. Father often works on accounts at home in the evenings. Older boy interested in photography.

d. If you have lived on a farm, or have visited one enough to be familiar with farm life, assume that one of these families lives on a farm typical of your locality. List the ways in which living on a farm affects family life, as opposed to town life. Collect plans of farmhouses, and select one that would be suitable for your family.

4. Find a plan for a large house that lends itself to building in sections.

READING REFERENCES

Blum, Milton, and Beatrice Candee. Family Behavior, Attitudes, and Possessions. John B. Pierce Foundation. New York. 1944.

Catlin, Mary, and George Catlin. Building Your New House. A. A. Wyn. New York. 1946.

Dunham, Clarence W. and Milton D. Thalberg. Planning Your Home for Better Living. McGraw-Hill Book Company, Inc. New York. 1945.

Ford, Katherine M. and Thomas H. Creighton. The American House Today. Reinhold Publishing Corporation. New York. 1954.

Pickering, Ernest. Shelter for Living. John Wiley and Sons, Inc. New York. 1950.

Walsh, H. V. Your House Begins with You. George W. Stewart, Inc. New York. 1950.

Chapter VI
A House Should Fit the Site

"But the glory of the house consisted in this, that there was a garden attached to it."

Anthony Trollope

So far we have dealt with the space inside of the house, with little reference to the lot on which it stands, chiefly because it is easier to begin that way. In actual practice, it is only sensible to find the best site you can afford, and then plan the house to fit it. In almost every way, the arrangement of interior space is dependent on the lot, and whatever advantages it offers as to view, orientation, and outdoor living. With a small lot, especially, it is necessary to think of the entire lot as living space, some of it indoor, and some outdoor, in order to get full returns of pleasant living on your investment.

Probably the commonest building site for a small house is a level inside lot, 50 to 60 feet wide, and 100 or so feet deep. In some overcrowded neighborhoods you will find lots that are considerably smaller than that, but they forfeit most of the advantages a detached house should have, such as privacy, light, air, and a place for outdoor living.

The direction toward which the lot faces is the first factor to be considered in planning a house to fit the site. It concerns the orientation of the house, that is, the arrangement of the rooms with regard to the points of the compass. A plan that is just right for a lot on the south side of the street is probably all wrong for one on the north side. The same thing is true to some degree of houses on the east and west sides of the street.

A general rule for modern orientation of a house is that the rooms with the largest window areas should go on the south side, while those areas that need little or no window space may be located on the north. This rule may be altered by local conditions of wind and climate, or the direction of the best view. It is for you to decide which rooms are most important in your house, but generally the living room and the bedrooms are considered worthy of the best exposure. Halls, stairs, bathrooms, closets, and garages are placed on the less desirable sides of the house.

The location of the kitchen depends on how much time you spend in it, and the use you intend to make of it. If it is a small room, used only for cooking, it might be slighted in its placing. But if you plan to have a large all-purpose kitchen, with space for dining and informal living, it deserves a good exposure. Winter sunshine is especially enjoyable in a room that is used so much during the day.

In Victorian times many women preferred a house that faced to the north. The reason was that then their parlor windows on the front could let in no sunshine to fade the plush sofa and the red roses in the carpet. Since then we have changed our attitude to sunshine in the house. We have learned how cheerful it can be on a cold day. The more permanent character of modern dyes has probably had something to do with the change. At any rate, the north-facing house is again in favor.

A house that faces to the north can have the living room at the back, where it may have large south windows without loss of privacy, and where the sunshine may pour in on winter days. Since all the better features of the exposure are found at the back of the house, a garage can be attached at the front or the side without destroying any of the desirable window space.

Another advantage of placing the living room at the back of the house is that the windows look out upon the rear of the lot, which may be developed into a pleasant view. When you build on a small lot, the only view you can control is that over your own land. Turning the house away from the street may pay dividends later on. You may build your house on a quiet suburban lane; not too many years later, expansion of the city may turn that lane into a noisy traffic artery. Placing the living room at the back was a rather shocking idea to many people not so long ago, but today plans of this type are generally accepted.

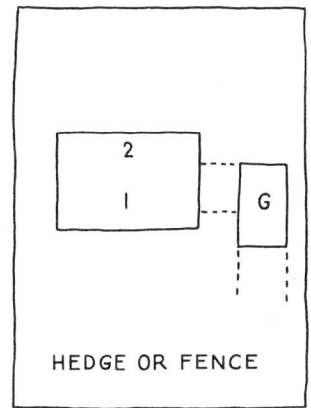

Figure 24 shows two arrangements that might be used for houses on the north and the south sides of a street. The best part of the interior space, in terms of orientation, is shown by the figure 1, while figure 2 indicates the less desirable part of the house. A small lot that faces to the south presents several difficulties for modern planning. If you use large glass areas on the south side, where they are best for sunshine and summer breeze, your rooms will lack privacy and your view will consist mainly of the street. A screen of shrubbery across the front of the lot will help in gaining privacy. Front fences and walls are acceptable in some localities, but would be resented as being un-neighborly in others. If you do not want to locate your outdoor living area in front of the house, one at the back, on the north side of the house, is satisfactory if it is easily accessible from indoors. An entrance to the garage from the back would be useful in a lot that faces south, but alleys are seldom used in newer neighborhoods because of their cost.

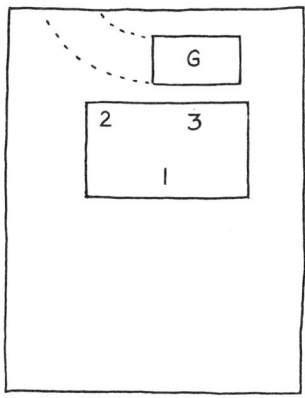

Figure 24

Lots facing
north and south.

If you want the greatest possible amount of southern exposure in a house that faces east or west, you will have to find a wide lot, and place the house endwise to the street, close to the north edge of the lot, as in Figure 25. Then the south windows may look out upon lawn space, and attractive planting that screens off the neighbor's house. The garage is placed on the north side of the house, where it affords shelter from winter winds.

It must be admitted that the arrangement described here is unfashionable at present. Most people seem to want their houses placed across the lot, to make them look larger from the street, even though the south windows are then too close

A HOUSE SHOULD FIT THE SITE

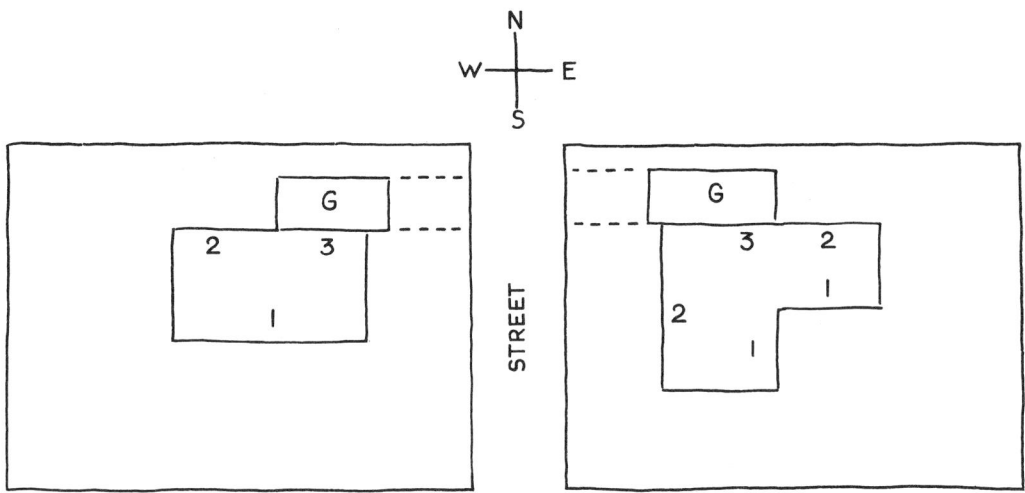

Figure 25

Lots facing east and west.

to the neighbor's house to be useful. Making a choice between fashion and the best orientation is not easy. It may help you to visit an older neighborhood and consider that those houses used to be top fashion in their day. Ten years from now today's houses may look old-fashioned in their turn.

A corner lot has both handicaps and advantages. The house is exposed on two sides to the noise and the lack of privacy of the street, but on the other hand there is greater flexibility in arranging the interior space, and in placing the garage. An L-shaped plan may be turned toward the interior of the lot, as in Figure 26, with relatively few windows on the street sides. A detached garage can be used as part of the enclosure for the outdoor living area, with a fenced walk to connect it with the house.

On irregular land, and in residential areas with curving streets, the lots are often triangular or wedge-shaped. The difficulties involved in using such lots are offset by the possibilities for greater freedom of arrangement. Houses may be set at varied angles to gain more privacy, better orientation, and unimpeded views from the windows on all sides. Figure 27 shows a section of a neighborhood with curving streets.

Because the plan of the house is so dependent on the site, it is well to find your building lot while your ideas on the kind of house you want are still flexible. A good location means a neighborhood with a well-established character, or at least a promising future. It also means congenial neighbors

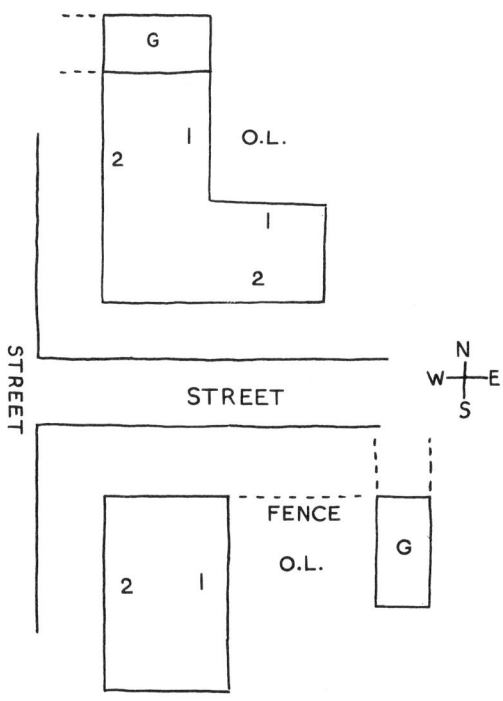

Figure 26

Corner lots.

whose social and economic level is similar to yours. Attractive visual surroundings, such as a pleasant view, trees, and ground formations that lend themselves to the development of lawns and gardens are also desirable. High ground is better drained and better ventilated than land in a valley. Level land is cheaper to build on, but a sloping site may offer a chance for an interesting split-level house.

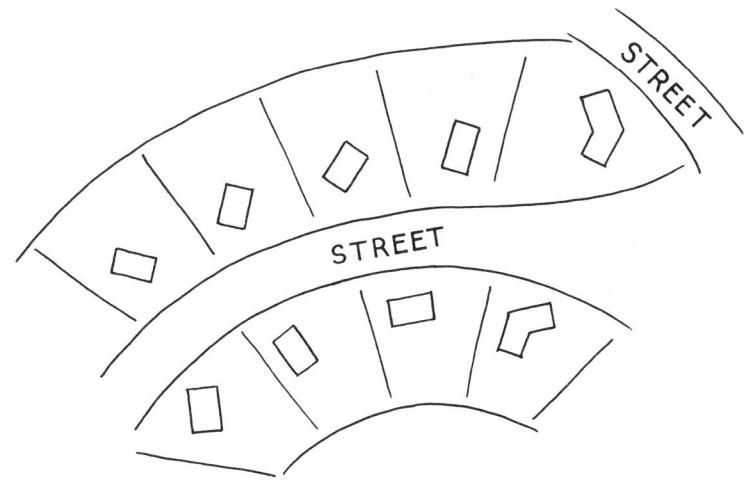

Figure 27

Lots on a curving street.

If street paving, sidewalks, sewers, and other utilities are in, they will be reflected in the cost of the lot. On the other hand, a cheap piece of land without these facilities may not be a bargain by the time that they are added. All special assessments for neighborhood improvements, such as storm sewers, should be investigated and counted in on the cost of the lot. Such services as transportation, fire and police protection, garbage and snow removal, should be investigated.

The future of the neighborhood is of great importance in the purchase of a lot. While it is not always possible to predict the development of a residential section, an estimate may be made from the existing restrictions, their probable duration, and the trends shown by the current growth of the town. Zoning laws are designed to prevent the invasion of residential districts by stores and factories, but such restrictions may be lifted, as a neighborhood changes.

Deed restrictions are more permanent in some cases. They often set a minimum price for houses to be build in a given neighborhood and a minimum size for lots. The object of such restrictions is the preservation of property values. Building a house in an unrestricted or a declining neighborhood may carry the penalty of unnaturally rapid depreciation in its value.

If you are looking for a building site in the country, beyond city water and sewer service, a reliable supply of safe water is of first importance. You cannot afford to be optimistic about the cost of digging a well, because water tables have been falling in many parts of the country. If you are unable to make certain of the water supply before you buy, reserve a generous share of your land cost for the well.

Second only to water for comfortable living in the country is reliable electric service. If the residents of the locality complain that the lights go out every time it thunders, the electrical service has probably not kept up with the population growth in the area.

Road maintenance is especially important where heavy rains or snows are the rule. Some country neighborhoods maintain a cooperative snow plough for driveways and back roads. Fire and police protection, mail and telephone service are needed in the country as well as in the city.

The decentralizing trend in industry and the growing number of non-farming country families have created a need for zoning restrictions in rural areas. A building site in a district reserved for residences has a secure future. Without rural zoning, your country house may in a few years have factory chimneys as a part of the view, or it may be surrounded by low-cost tract houses.

It is hardly necessary to mention the depth of your purse as a factor in your choice of a lot. Naturally there is a relationship between the total amount of money you can spend and the value of the lot. If your income justifies a large costly house, it is only sensible to build it on a lot that, in size and location, is good enough for the house, and if your budget is limited a small house on an inexpensive lot will have to do.

It is better to spend too much on the lot, rather than too little. That is, you take a greater risk in building a costly house on a too-small or a badly located lot, than you would investing a fairly large proportion of your money in an excellent lot, and building a smaller house that could be expanded later.

The choice of where you want to live must be made on the basis of your needs and preferences. You must weigh the advantages against the drawbacks, and decide what you want most. The spacious suburban lot means a long ride twice a day for the city worker, with pleasant weekends as compensation. The convenience of living close to work or school may call for a small lot in a closely built neighborhood.

If you enjoy gardening, and look forward to having a lavish display of flowers, it would be better not to buy a heavily wooded lot, for flowers grow unwillingly under trees. It might be mentioned here that trees may be enjoyed without being owned; they will delight your eyes whether they stand on your own land or your neighbors'. A treeless lot in a wooded neighborhood is usually cheaper than the lots with trees on them.

The modern use of large glass areas in houses has made all of conscious of the need for attractive views to be seen through them. Everybody wants a site with a view. But before you buy be sure that your view is a lasting one. If your lot lies on the edge of town you may at first see a lovely sweep across fields and hills. A few years later the lot just beyond yours may be sold, and then your picture windows will probably look out upon the new neighbor's garage.

In general, the only view you can count on is the one over your own land, unless you have a very high location. If you cannot afford to buy a large acreage, then your own lot, carefully planted and tended, will offer a view that will be pleasant, if not spacious.

If you are building on your own, it is wise to get in touch with an architect early, so that he may advise you on the final choice of a building site. His experience will enable him to see, better than you can, which site will serve as the best location for the kind of house you want.

After a satisfactory lot has been found, and the price agreed upon, the next step is to employ a lawyer or a title company to investigate the title to the property. A title search is usually not costly, and should by no means be neglected. If the owner cannot give you a clear title to the property, do not buy it. Serious trouble may develop later if there are flaws in the title record. It is the seller's duty to provide a clear title, but the buyer must find the points that need clearing. Unpaid taxes, errors in the spelling of names, and incorrect descriptions of boundaries are some of the usual title flaws. Investigate also any possible easements which give others the right to cross or use the property.

If the boundaries of the land are in doubt, a survey should be made before building is started. It is embarrassing to find after a few years that your garage and driveway lie partly on your neighbor's land, and almost as painful to discover that you have made him a present of expensive shrubs by planting them beyond the lot line.

With a building enterprise of any great size and cost, it is practically necessary to enlist the help of a landscape architect. He will advise you as to the placing of the house on the lot for the best orientation and views, and the future development of the exterior space.

If you are building a small house on a small lot, and expect to do your own exterior planning, it is useful to draw the plan of the lot on a large piece of paper. Wrapping paper will do, and a yardstick will help you work out the scale. After the outline of the lot has been drawn, mark the points of the compass, the direction of the prevailing breeze in summer, the existing trees and other planting, and the direction of the best view. If the lot slopes, the fall of the land should be shown. Then note any disadvantages, such as a neighbor's house too close to the lot line, or an untidy service yard. Mark the direction from which winter storm, or sandstorms, or other unpleasant manifestations of nature can be expected to come. Note also the restrictions to which the lot is subject, such as the minimum space required in front of and at each side of the house, and any restrictions as to the placing of the garage.

After the lot plan is drawn, cut out another piece of paper in the approximate size of the house, and try it in various positions on the lot. Be sure that the house pattern is in the same scale as the lot, so that you will not have any illusions as to the amount of space at your disposal.

It is a good thing at this point to go outdoors and do some actual measuring around the house you live in now. Measure the length and width of your present driveway, the distance between your house and the next-door neighbor's, and how far the house is from the street. We are quite likely to misjudge outdoor space. A ten-foot strip beside the house may look adequate on paper, but when you measure it outdoors you will find that is very narrow. The sense of space mentioned in Chapter 2 can be developed for outdoor measurements as well as for those within the house, and will be of great value in planning your lot.

EXERCISES

1. Draw the lot plan of your own home, or of one belonging to a friend. List the good and bad points you find in it.

2. Draw a lot plan based on an actual building site in your community, following the directions in the text. Show the best orientation, the view, and any disadvantages it may have. Indicate the best position of the house on the lot, and the outdoor living area.

3. In your collection of plans clipped from magazines there will be some that include the lot plan. Look them over and select the one you consider the best; list its good points and also any faults you may find. You may have to sketch it in a larger scale.

4. Visit a residential section of your town, and note the houses that are well placed on the lot, as well as those in which some advantage has been wasted. How many garages are located on the south side of the house? Look for unusual sites, such as sloping ground and lots of odd shape and note the ways in which they have been used.

READING REFERENCES

Goldsmith, Margaret O. Designs for Outdoor Living. George W. Stewart. New York. 1941.

Ormsbee, Thomas H. and Richmond Huntley. If You're Going to Live in the Country. Thomas Y. Crowell Company. New York. 1937.

Ortloff, H. Stuart, and Henry B. Raymore. Garden Planning and Building. McGraw-Hill Book Company, Inc. New York. 1939.

Van de Boe, L. Planning and Planting Your Own Place. The Macmillan Company. New York. 1938.

Sunset Magazine. Outdoor Building Book. Lane Publishing Company. Menlo Park, California. 1953.

Chapter VII
A House Should Fit the Climate

"If one is going to have the right kind of house, one must plan to have it comfortable....it must be cool in summer and warm in winter....one must build the part facing the south higher, in order that the sun may not be shut out; and the part facing the north one must build lower, that the cold winds may not blow in."

Socrates   (Xenophon)

Houses of today need not reflect the local climate so directly in their design as did those of earlier times, thanks to modern developments in construction and equipment. The early colonial houses of New England, for instance, with their steep roofs, low ceilings, and compact shape, bear witness to the severe winters of the region, as well as to the inefficiency of the fireplaces that were their only source of heat.

Today, double-glazed windows, insulation, and modern heating systems have made the design of houses quite independent of the weather. We see sprawling one-story houses with glass walls and flat roofs throughout the northern part of the country, as well as in warmer sections. Cooling systems, window and attic fans, and electric dehumidifiers contribute to comfort in hot weather. It might be noted, however, that all this equipment adds considerably to the first cost of building, as well as to the running expenses of a house. Defiance of the weather is not cheap.

Insulation, storm sash, and weather-stripping may be regarded as an investment. They will pay for themselves through the years by saving fuel. The same thing may be said of the rather costly double glazing of large glass areas, for, in addition to saving heat, it also prevents condensation moisture from forming on the inner surface of the glass in cold weather.

As a part of your study of plans, it is well to analyze the weather conditions under which you live, as they may affect the plan or the construction of the house. In many parts of the country the weather is so variable that it is not easy to classify. Perhaps the most difficult climate to plan for is that of some parts of the middle west, where extremes of both heat and cold occur during the year. However, if you must keep the heating plant going as much as eight months of the year, yours is a winter climate, even though periods of heat occur during the summer.

If you cannot afford to spend money freely in ignoring the weather, you may adjust the plan of your house to fit the climate. For economical winter comfort, a compact rectangular plan offers less outside wall space to the weather in proportion to the floor area. Small rooms with low ceilings are more easily heated. Large openings between rooms and open stairways, on the other hand, may create drafts. Vestibules, especially on the side of the prevailing winter winds, prevent heat loss when doors are opened. An attached garage on the windward side of the house is useful to break the force of winter storms. In country locations, windbreaks of evergreen trees are valuable aids to winter comfort.

As for large windows and glass walls, their location determines whether or not they will be a financial liability. On the south side of the house they let in enough heat on sunny days in winter to compensate for that lost at other times, provided that they are covered by substantial curtains at night. The cost of curtains, however, is a sizeable item of expense if you have large glass areas.

If you live in a part of the country where the periods of hot weather are not long enough to justify the expense of cooling equipment, there are a number of ways to cope with the heat. Light-colored roofing that reflects the sun's heat, insulation, and a well-ventilated attic, all help to keep a house cool. The plan can be oriented so that the prevailing summer breeze is directed through the house. Hot dry winds by day combined with cooling off at night are best dealt with by closing the house early in the day and opening it in the late afternoon, just as our grandmothers used to do. A window or attic fan to draw in the cooler outside air is especially useful when the breeze dies down at sunset.

Closing the house by day is less effective when summer discomfort is caused more by humidity than by heat. The traditional practice in humid climates has been to provide for a constant flow of air through the house. Casement windows are good for this purpose, because they allow 100% opening. Awning-type windows are useful where frequent showers occur in warm weather. Here again, nature may be helped by attic fans and electric dehumidifiers. The latter, however, are effective only when the house is closed against outdoor humidity.

Cooling equipment, commonly called air-conditioning, may be a part of a warm-air heating system, or a separate unit. Planning for summer cooling is a highly technical subject, and not all the problems have been solved. It involves fending off as much outdoor heat, from the sun and hot winds, as possible. The methods of keeping a house cool, as mentioned above, are also useful in connection with cooling equipment.

In cities, where paved streets and masonry walls store up heat, cooling systems are especially welcome. In the country, the tightly closed house and the fixed windows advocated by air-conditioning manufacturers would deprive us of some of the simple pleasures of rural life, such as the scent of flowers in the garden, the songs of birds, and the fresh sweet air after a storm.

The large glass areas that are such a pleasant feature of modern houses need to be shielded from the sun in hot weather. Curtains and venetian blinds on the inside are not efficient in this respect, because they do not keep the sun's heat from touching the glass and being passed on by conduction to the air within the house. The shading device must be outside the glass.

Awnings, shutters, trellises, and wide overhangs of the roof are all used to shield windows from the sun. Permanent awnings of wood or metal are widely advertised, but they cut off the light from the upper half of the window. You might not mind this in summer, when a darkened room gives an illusion of coolness, but in winter it is another story. If you like daylight better than lamplight, you will not willingly throw it away. Permanent awnings also cut off your view of the sky. Being able to see the sky from indoors is another simple pleasure that adds to our enjoyment of life.

Figure 28

A wide roof overhang is visible from indoors.

Wide roof overhangs are now used as a part of the fashionable design known as "ranch-style". They are most useful in the south, but in the northern states they can mean darkened rooms in winter. A uniform wide overhang all around the house is open to question. It is most useful on the south side, where it cuts off the sun's rays in summer but allows them to enter in winter, when the sun is low in the sky.

On the east and west side, a wide overhang is only partly useful, for it cannot shield the windows from the sun in the early morning or late afternoon. On the north side, sunshine is a minor problem, although some heat is reflected from the sky. Usually, however, the windows on the north side of a house are few in number and small in size.

You may enjoy the freedom from glare afforded by a wide overhang above a glass wall in the living room, but that same overhang will cut off too much light from the little high windows currently used in bedrooms. Anyone who has lived in an old-time bungalow knows the darkening effect of an overhang that is too low in regard to the windows. Furthermore, if it is neglected, peeling paint and grime can make it an unsightly part of the view.

An overhang that is kept well above the windows will avoid these drawbacks. The upper edges of shed and butterfly roofs, since they slant up away from the house, interfere less with the lighting of a room than do overhangs of gable and hip roofs.

In some modern houses we see roof extensions that are not solid. They may be made of wood strips, slanted to deflect the sun's rays without cutting off too much daylight. In other houses wide overhangs are built with openings in them, as in Figure 29. If you wonder why people have overhangs so wide that they must cut holes in them to let in the daylight, the answer is that wide roofs enhance the horizontal effect

Figure 29

A partially open overhang lets in a little light.

that is so fashionable now. Another question that is harder to answer is why a house should have any kind of "effect".

Deciduous trees have always been used to provide shade for houses, and they have many advantages over man-made shade. Fast-growing trees on the east and west sides of a house will begin to give summer comfort in just a few years, and take care of the late afternoon and early morning sunshine that overhangs cannot control. A tree off the south-west corner of the house shades the ground to the south, preventing glare and heat from being reflected into south windows.

Trees that have been trimmed to grow tall before branching out will give shade without cutting off the breeze. Since fast-growing trees are often short-lived, more durable, slower-growing species may be set out nearby to take over the job of shading in later years. Where lots are narrow, your neighbors' trees will give you some of the shade you need.

The location of the garage and the outdoor living area have some bearing on summer comfort. The garage should not be located where it interferes with the prevailing summer breeze. A paved driveway or terrace can reflect a good deal of heat toward the house unless it is shaded. Even if you use a paved terrace mostly in the evenings, it needs shade, otherwise it will store up enough heat to be uncomfortably warm after dark.

In those parts of the country where heavy rainfall is common, the plan may include shelter for all outside entrances, with storage for rainwear and a place to sit down when dealing with overshoes. Paving for all approaches to the house will cut down on the amount of mud tracked into the house. Large windows are useful to offset the gloomy, closed-in feeling of rooms when you must spend much time indoors. For outdoor living, paved terraces under the sky need to be supplemented by covered porches for use on rainy days.

The question of a screened porch is closely related to the climate. It might be considered a luxury in cool climates, where it is used for only a couple of months out of the year, but in warmer sections it is almost a necessity for comfortable living, especially where insects and frequent showers limit the use of a terrace.

Placing a porch is not a simple problem. In order to justify the expense, it should be so easily accessible from inside the house that it will be in constant use during the summer. The adjoining room should not be darkened by having its principal windows open onto the porch. Since a living porch needs privacy to be fully useful, it should be sheltered from the street, and front-door traffic should not pass through it. These requirements show why the old-time front porch has been discarded. The long narrow shape of the front porch was another handicap. To be useful as a room, a porch should be room-shaped.

As to orientation, east, west, or north porches are usually better than one on the south side of the house, because they do not cut off too much winter sunshine from the room behind. The breezeway, or porch between house and garage, is useful as a summer dining room, because it is usually near the kitchen. Like all through openings, it draws in whatever breeze may be stirring, hence its name. Sometimes the garage itself is built with removable wall panels, so that it may serve as a screened porch during the summer months, when the car can get along without shelter.

The climate has something to do with the use of basements, but modern materials and equipment have altered conditions. For example, in warm humid climates condensation moisture on walls and floors used to make basements all but useless; this problem is met by the use of electric dehumidifiers. In cold climates, a heated basement used to be considered necessary for winter comfort upstairs, but now newer types of heating equipment and floor insulation have made the house independent of the basement.

Other factors affect the basement question. It is best omitted when the house is to stand on poorly drained soil, or where underground water is present, or on rock that would require expensive blasting. In cold climates where foundations must go deep anyhow, the extra cost of excavating a full basement may not be too great, and the space gained is relatively cheap, compared with above-ground building costs. On sloping ground at least a part of the basement is likely to be above ground, and may be used as living space.

If you are not too familiar with local conditions that affect the use of basements, the general practice of the region is some sort of guide. You can study the methods used by reliable builders in the community and ask for information from people who have lived there a long time.

If you decide that it would be better not to have a basement under your house, you have your choice of two ways of building the foundation. One is called slab construction. A concrete platform is poured on the ground, and the house is erected on it. The other method is to run the foundations a foot or so above ground level before placing the first floor, using a shallow excavation beneath, called crawl space. The success of either method depends upon thorough insulation of the floor against cold, and protection against ground moisture that rises up through the soil by capillary action and then passes through the floor as vapor. Vapor can travel through concrete and wood. It can be stopped by asphalt, metal, and some plastics. In slab construction a vapor barrier is laid down under the concrete. Naturally it must be permanent, since it cannot be replaced without tearing the house down. When crawl space is used, the vapor barrier may be placed on the under side of the floor. Here again it is useful to study the ways in which local builders handle this problem.

EXERCISES

1. Study your own home in terms of the climate. Is it uncomfortable from heat, cold, humidity, or any other causes connected with the weather? Study the advertising pages of building magazines, listing materials and equipment that could improve the house.

2. Select a part of the country in which you are interested, and collect plans and pictures of houses built in that region; note the ways in which they meet local weather conditions.

Chapter VIII
Two-story Houses

"Houses are built to live in, not to look on."
Francis Bacon

During the past 15 years, two-story houses have been eclipsed in popularity by one-story houses. This fact can be seen, not only in the low-cost tract house, but also in large custom-built houses. A generation or two ago it used to be taken for granted that large houses were to be on two or more floors, and one-story houses were thought of as cottages. In those days some of the better residential neighborhoods even had restrictions forbidding one-story houses.

Figure 30

The small Colonial house, a favorite of yesterday.

There are certain advantages in a two-story house. It is more economical to build, because foundation and roof costs are lower, compared with the same space on one floor. It is easier to plan than a one-story house, because it has twice as many corner rooms. If you want a fairly large house on a small lot, the only way to get it is to put some of the space upstairs. Second floor bedrooms enjoy more privacy and quiet than do those on the first floor. The principal objection to the two-story house is the need for climbing stairs. It is a valid objection, for stairs cause a large proportion of home accidents. Maintenance jobs, also, such as painting and changing screens, are more difficult and hazardous in a two-story house.

If you prefer all your rooms on one level, but for some reason must build a two-story house, you may be reconciled to it by an extra room and a bath or lavatory on the first floor. The extra room may serve as an all-purpose room; sewing and odd jobs of mending are more likely to be done if they can be picked up between kitchen chores, than if you must run upstairs to do them. Children can use the extra room for play, and later for study and recreation. If a grandparent is taken into the family, the room may be converted into a bedroom, since many older people find it difficult to climb stairs.

While the traditional arrangement of two-story houses places the living area on the first floor, and bedrooms and bath on the second, some conditions might call for the reverse. If the lot slopes down from the street the living area might be above, and the bedrooms below. A water-side house, where the climate permits a long swimming season, might have the bedrooms and bath on the ground level, so that swimmers may come in and dress without tracking sand through the house.

Every discussion of economy in building mentions placing the bathroom over the kitchen, and lining up partitions, one above the other. You will have to balance the unquestioned savings effected by such arrangement, against what it does to the plan. If the saving is not obtained without spoiling the size and shape of a room, or its orientation, it is hardly worth having. Sometimes it is better to spend extra money on plumbing and carpenter work in order to obtain the best use of the second floor space. A compromise can usually be worked out by keeping at least some of the partitions in line, and grouping the plumbing fixtures in the same general area of the house.

While the stairway is important, it may be regarded as one of the lesser features of the house in regard to orientation. Together with the halls, it is a utility, providing circulation through the house. The actual rooms are more deserving of southern exposure and the view. In fact, the stairway can get along without a window, with electric light switches at top and bottom.

The shape and placing of the stairway depend on the space that can be allowed for it after the more important areas are taken care of. If there is a separate entrance hall, the stairway usually leads up from it. When, for the sake of economy, the entrance hall and also a hall space at the foot of the steps are omitted, the stairway leads up from one of the downstairs rooms, usually the living room. The price you pay for this economy is the possibility of drafts in winter, and extra traffic through the living room, as well as less privacy.

The top of the stairway is more important in terms of planning than the bottom, for it must lead to a hall from which all the bedrooms may open. Often the stairs seem to fit nicely into the first floor plan, only to require too much hall space upstairs. This means that both floors of a two-story house must be planned together. While no general rule for placing the stairway can be made, it is safe to say that the plan is more likely to work out well upstairs when the top steps lead toward the middle of the house. This places the hall in the central area, and leaves the more desirable corner spaces for rooms.

The general tendency today is to treat the stairway very simply, as a convenience, even in the larger houses. In older times the stairway was regarded as an important decorative feature of the interior, as we can see in the graceful elaborate staircases of Georgian and Greek Revival mansions, the older Elizabethan and Jacobean houses of England, and the French chateaux and manor houses.

Several arrangements of small two-story houses are shown in Figure 31-a-b-c. The dotted lines in the stairways indicate the spaces that can be used above the bottom steps and below a few at the top. Plan A represents one of the most used arrangements, with a straight stairway up the center. It is commonly called a colonial plan, because it lends itself to a central doorway and formally balanced front windows. A central-stairway plan is useful when the principal rooms are at the front of the house. In plans B and C, the rear of the house is a more favorable exposure, with the stairway and less important rooms at the front.

On hillside lots, houses may be built on varying levels. The split-level house is more acceptable to many people than one with two full stories, because the stair runs between adjoining sections are shorter. Probably the reason for the growing popularity of hillside houses lies in the development of modern architecture. Traditional design no longer lays a restraining hand on the appearance of

TWO-STORY HOUSES

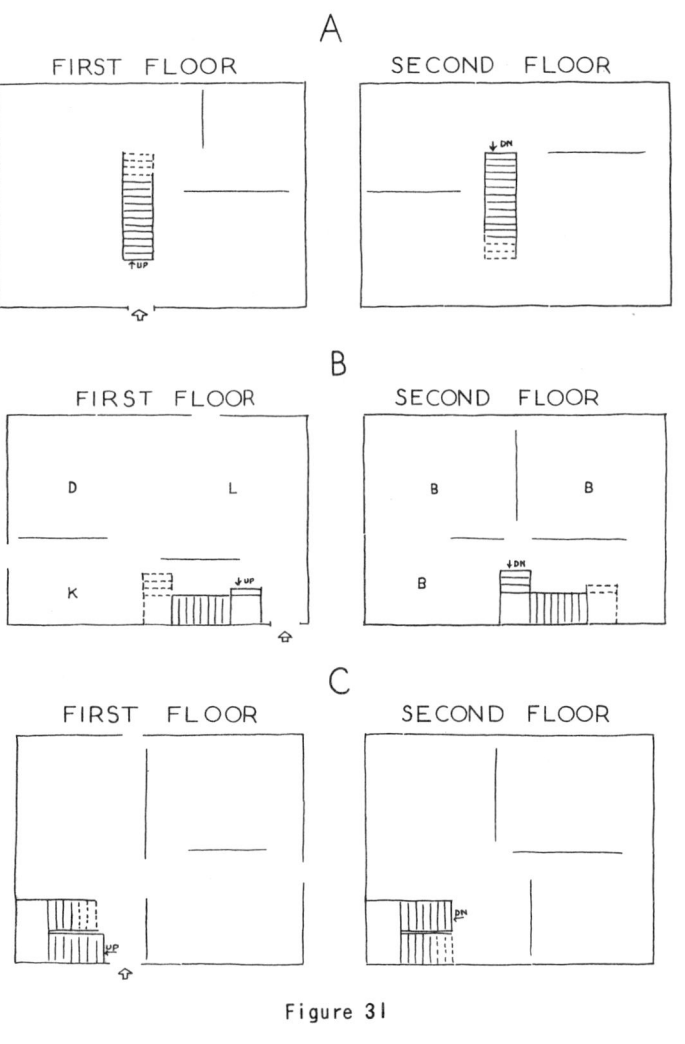

Figure 31

Two-story plans.

houses. A house need not look like a Georgian mansion or a French chateau. It need only look like itself, so long as it is a logical, unified design. A modern house can step down a hillside or project boldly from a cliff, or straddle a ravine, if you can afford the construction features needed to make it secure.

A few of the many possibilities in arranging hillside houses are shown in Figure 32. A is not really a split-level house, but one in which the rear half of the basement is far enough above ground to be used for living quarters.

B shows the same general arrangement, in a true split-level house, with the garage and entrance hall on an intermediate level, the living rooms down a half flight of steps and the bedrooms above. The entrance hall can serve also as the landing of the staircase.

In C the lot is approached from below. The garage is on the lowest level, with the bedrooms above it, while the living area is on the intermediate level.

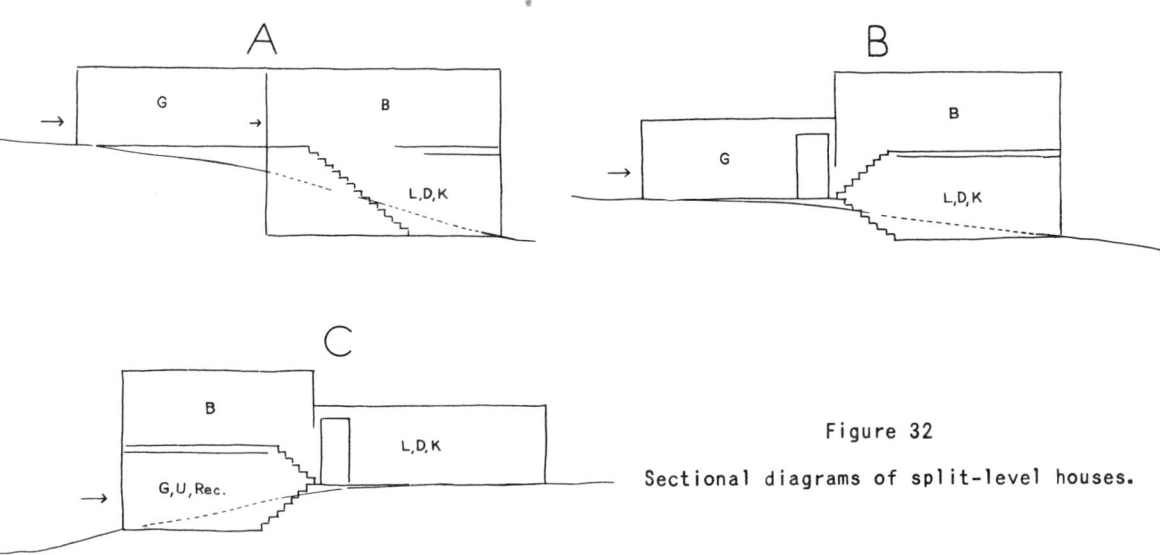

Figure 32

Sectional diagrams of split-level houses.

TWO-STORY HOUSES

Figure 33

A split-level house.

Figure 34

A hillside house makes use of part of the basement space.

EXERCISES

1. In order to judge two-story houses, you will need a little general knowledge of stairway planning. The amount of space needed for a stairway depends on the height of the ceiling and the steepness of the stairs. The latter is related to the height and width of the individual step, called the riser and the tread, respectively.

   A simple rule for the proportion of a step is that tread and riser together should measure about 17-1/2 inches. This figure represents a comfortable step for the average adult. If the tread is wide, the riser must be low. Such steps are easy to climb, but they may take too much space for a small house. At the other extreme, tall narrow steps are tiring to climb and dangerous on the descent. Folding attic steps are steep and narrow. You can tolerate them occasionally, but not for everyday use. For a small house we must find a proportion of riser and tread that combines economy of space with reasonable comfort. See Figure 35. Such a step is between 9 and 11 inches wide and 7 to 8 inches high.

   To find the height of the riser divide the total height (ceiling plus thickness of flooring) by the number of steps that will probably be used. In a small house this number will be 14, 15, or 16, depending on the height of the ceiling. Subtract the riser from 17-1/2 to find the width of the tread.

   The most helpful exercise for the amateur is to make a scale drawing of a stairway, showing the relationship between its plan and a vertical section, as in Figure 36.

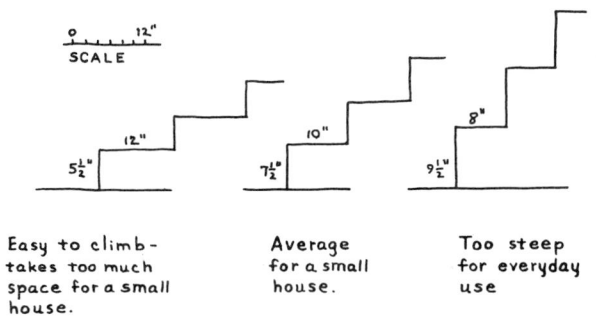

Easy to climb - takes too much space for a small house.

Average for a small house.

Too steep for everyday use

Figure 35

Risers and treads.

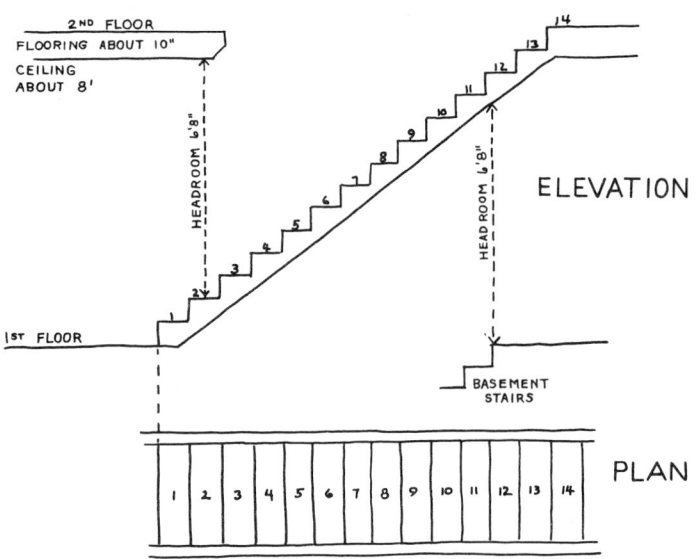

Figure 36

Plan and elevation of a stairway.

1. A little space may be retrieved from the stairway and used in the plan, because you can walk under the top few steps, and extend the second floor over a few feet from the bottom. These spaces are marked "headroom" in the illustration.

   Any step may be widened to make a landing if the plan calls for a stairway that turns. Figure 37 shows some commonly used stairways that turn. Winders, or steps on the turn, save a little space, but they are to be avoided because they are dangerous.

2. Select a two-story plan from your collection of clippings, that is especially suited to your own family. Copy it to scale, place the furniture, and list its good and bad points, according to Ex. 1, Chapter 5.

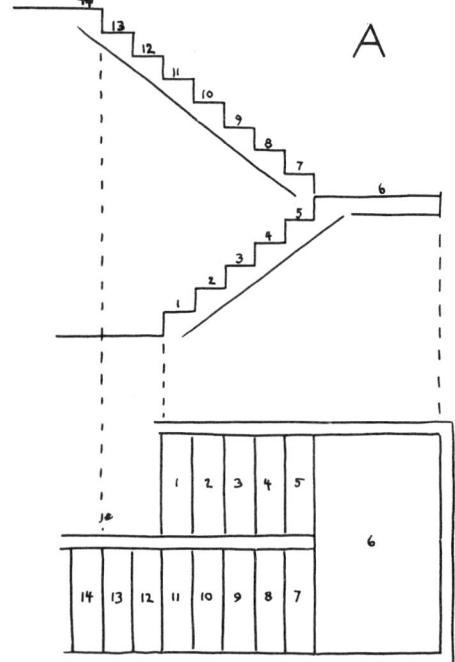
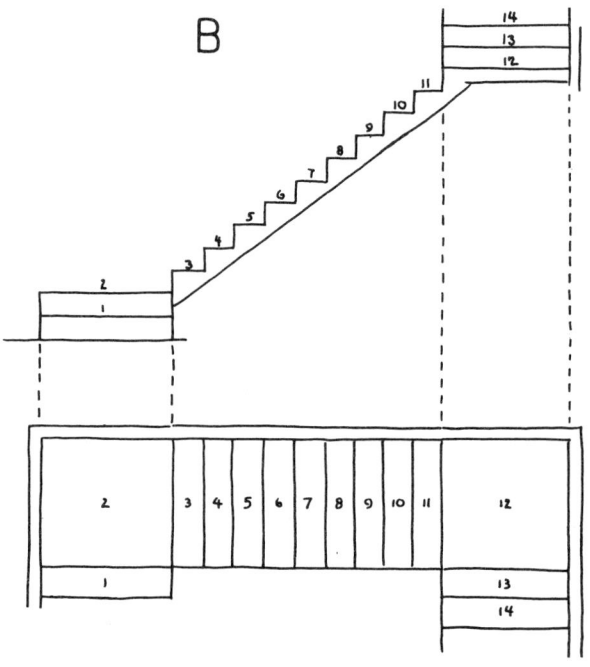

Figure 37

Landings and turns.

3. Using one of the arrangements in Figure 29, draw a plan to scale for a two-story house.

4. Starting with a vertical section as in Figure 33, plan a split-level house. Try to find an actual building site in your community as the basis for your plan.

READING REFERENCES

Duncan, Kenneth. <u>Primer for Home Builders and Home Buyers</u>. Funk & Wagnalls Company. New York. 1947.

Chapter IX
Story-and-a-half Houses

"The best way to realize the pleasure of feeling rich is to live in a smaller house than your means would entitle you to have."
Edward Clarke

During the 1930's the story-and-a-half Cape Cod cottage enjoyed widespread popularity. Its white clapboard walls, green shutters, and rather steep roof are a familiar sight in the not-quite-new residential sections of any town.

Since that time the Cape Cod cottage has been superseded in public favor by flatter-roofed one-story houses. Even the name has gone out of fashion. When story-and-a-half houses are built they are spoken of as "expansion-attic" houses. The new term is justified because in many instances the colonial details have been discarded. Modern fenestration and doorway design have given the house a new look.

Figure 38

A Cape Cod cottage.

The expansion-attic house is just what the name implies; a one-story house with a roof steep enough to provide an attic that may be made into one or two rooms. These extra rooms make about the least expensive way of adding to a house, because they do not require any construction of extra foundation, roof, or exterior wall. Finishing interior surfaces is a fairly simple job that can be done by the owner himself. If plumbing connections are put in when the house is built an extra bathroom can be installed upstairs without excessive cost.

The amount of usable space in an attic must be of room size, or at least 10 feet wide, if it is to be used for rooms. "Usable" space might be defined as space in which an adult can stand upright. The main problem in planning attic rooms is to arrange the space so that you will not bump your head on the slanting ceiling. This means keeping all traffic lines a foot or two in from the lowest part of the ceiling.

The size of the second floor depends on the width of the first floor and the slope of the roof. In Figure 39 the upstairs bedrooms are the same width in both houses, but the narrower house (B) must have an extremely steep roof to provide that space. The area of roof would also be greater and more expensive, if we assume that the first floors of the two houses cover the same area. Steep roofs were well liked during the 1920's, when the picturesque old English and Norman houses were fashionable, but now they look rather strange to eyes accustomed to the flattened-out ranch style of recent years.

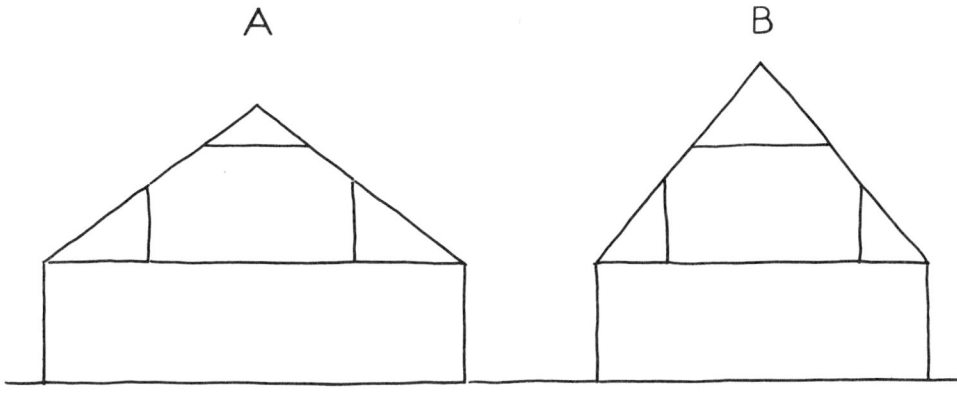

Figure 39

Second floor space is related to the size of the house and the slope of the roof.

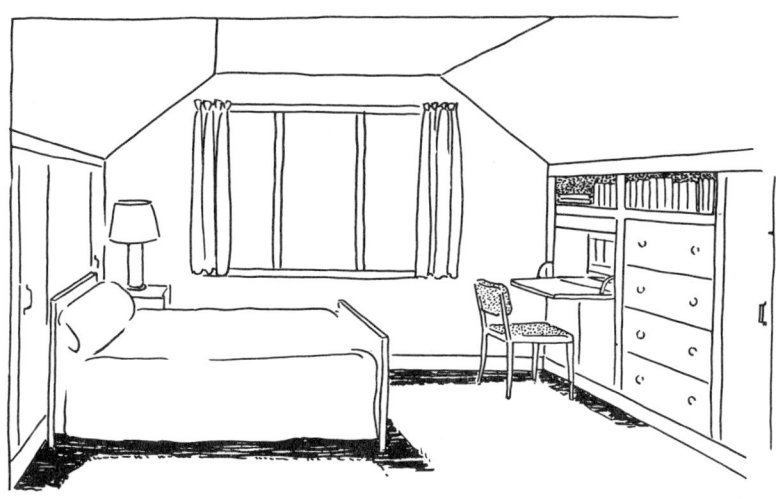

Figure 40

Space under the eaves may be used for built-in furniture.

The ceiling of attic rooms is usually full height across the central part, but slopes down to a height of 5 or 6 feet at the sides. It is useless to extend the ceiling farther down than this to gain more floor space. You can gain only bumps on your head. The low triangular spaces at the sides may be used for storage and built-in furniture, as shown in Figure 40.

Since the roof covers two sides of the attic space, windows can be used only in the ends of the house, unless dormers are cut in the roof. Windows in a sidewall are cheaper than dormers; therefore the most economical type of plan makes use of the ends of the attic space for bedrooms, keeping the stairway and storage areas toward the center of the house.

56 STORY-AND-A-HALF HOUSES

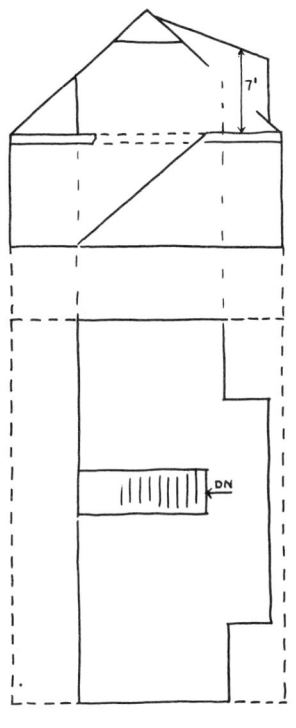

Figure 41

A shed dormer adds to second floor space.

In many houses the second floor space is supplemented by a shed dormer. Shed dormers have never enjoyed a very good social position, and are usually hidden away on the back of the house. It is a good idea to limit the width and height of such a dormer, so that it will not be out of proportion to the house itself. Figure 41 shows the additional space that can be gained with a shed dormer on the rear of a house.

Figure 42 shows the simplest arrangement for an expansion-attic plan, with a straight stairway across the center of the house. The three parts of the drawing are connected by dotted lines to show the relationship between the first floor, a vertical section through the middle of the house, and the second floor. This plan is wide enough to provide ample head-room on the top landing. If the house were narrow, that headroom would have to be provided by a shed dormer as mentioned above.

Another type of plan is shown in Figure 43. Here the house is oriented toward the rear. The roof itself serves as the ceiling for the landing and the upper part of the stairway.

EXERCISES

1. Look for examples of story-and-a-half houses in current magazines. Compare them with one-story houses of the same number of rooms, as to size of foundation, convenience, and cost.

2. Study the exterior designs of these houses. Note the ways in which their details differ from those of the conventional Cape Cod house.

3. Using one of the stairway arrangements shown in the illustrations, develop a plan for a story-and-a-half house.

STORY-AND-A-HALF HOUSES

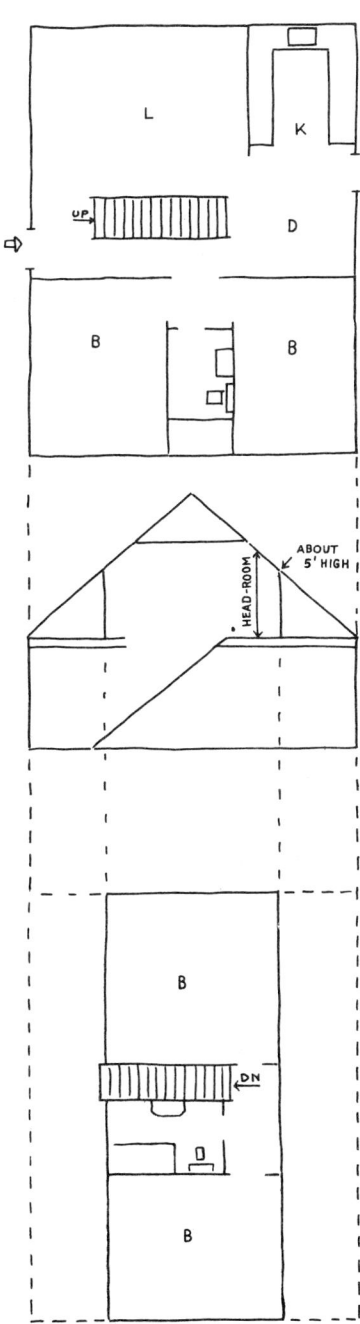

Figure 42

Relation of elevation to first and second floors.

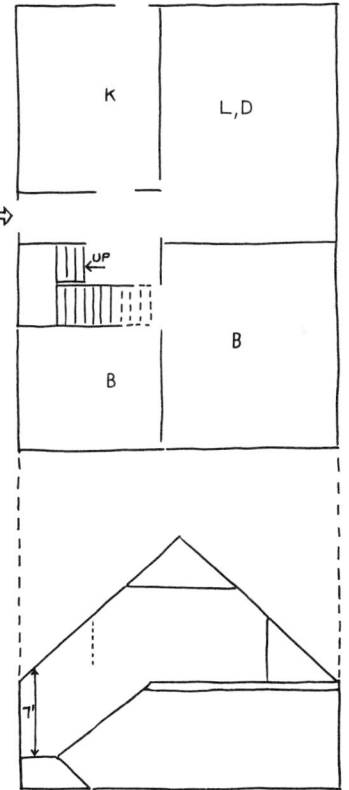

Figure 43

Another 1½-story plan.

Chapter X
Remodeling an Old House

"Old houses mended,
Cost little less than new,
Before they're ended."
                    Colley Cibber

Sometimes the best answer to your housing problem is to buy an old house and remodel it. There are several requirements that a house must meet to make it worth buying. First, the selling price must be low enough so that you can afford to make the necessary repairs and alterations. For this you would have to obtain an estimate from a building contractor on the cost of the remodeling.

Second, the structure must be sound. The contractor will be able to tell you if the foundations and the important parts of the frame are good enough to justify your purchase. Certain flaws are so fundamental that they can scarcely be remedied, but the average untrained person is not likely to find them.

Third, the house must be in a good location. This you may find out for yourself, by looking at the surroundings, and by finding out what restrictions there are to prevent encroachment by factories and stores. In a city, the general trend of the neighborhood may be seen in the other old houses nearby. If they are being reclaimed as private residences, the future looks good; if they are being turned into shops and rooming houses, it would be risky to set up a permanent residence there.

Another requirement is harder to define, for it concerns you. While the contractor is looking at the house, take a look at yourself. Will it make you unhappy to live in an old house, when your friends are building new ones that are the latest style? Do you like old houses well enough to put up with some of their infirmities, such as floors that are not quite level, stairs that creak, and doors that must be coaxed to stay shut?

Most important of all, are you willing to leave the house as it is? If your reason for buying it is economy, you cannot afford to tear it apart and rebuild it. You must be careful not to let the old house eat up as much as you would have spent on a new one. You can adjust your thinking so that you can take an old house as it is, instead of trying to make a new one out of it.

Before you decide to buy an old house, you will want to find out if it can be altered to suit your needs. Some of the preliminary work you can do yourself, but for the final plans, as in building a new house, it is best to employ an architect.

The kind of remodeling you do depends on the type and condition of the house. If the house is so old and dilapidated that extensive repairs must be made, structural changes may be made at the same time, at slight extra cost. On the other hand, if the house is in good condition, drastic changes in structure might be too extravagant.

Probably the best way to remodel a house is to do as little rebuilding as possible, other than repair. Justifiable changes that add to the value of the house are such things as the addition of bathrooms and storage space, putting in new windows, and sometimes adding entirely new rooms. Minor changes, such as removing a partition between two small rooms to make a large one, or dividing a long room, are also reasonable. Moving stairways and plumbing fixtures is relatively expensive, but the cost may be balanced by a more convenient and pleasant house.

Since you will probably want to add electric equipment, the wiring system will probably not be equal to the demands that you will make on it. It needs to be thoroughly examined, and probably replaced. The cost of doing this is not so great as a fire caused by inadequate wiring.

Some features, such as rooms that are too small, or displeasing in shape or proportion, often cannot be corrected without great expense. Perhaps you can be reconciled to them by the low cost of the house, or some other advantage. Many faults in room design may be disguised by artful color schemes, window draping, and the choice and arrangement of furniture.

Old houses often fail to measure up to modern standards as to bathrooms and storage space. Sometimes a small bedroom may be converted into a couple of bathrooms, or into a bath and several closets. If a new partition is added anywhere in the house, it may well take the form of a storage wall. When new closets must be added to the existing structure, wide shallow cupboards along an entire side of the room will look better than square closets cut out of a corner. The extra width often found in the hallways of old houses can also be used for shallow storage.

Old houses were planned for older ways of living; they reflect the custom of spending most of the time indoors, and the separation of the house into two parts: the front for the family and the rear for the servants. To bring an old house into line with modern servantless, outdoor living, it might be a good thing to turn the plan around. If the kitchen and pantry have southern exposure and command a view of the garden, they may form the new living room, while the new kitchen may be fitted into a front room. Such a change will also bring the outdoor and indoor living areas closer together. Changing neighborhood conditions, such as increased traffic, may also have made the front of the house less attractive for a living room.

It is wise to let changes in the exterior design wait upon the development of the interior. You may even want to live in the house for a few years before deciding on the complete remodeling plan. In the meantime, the outside appearance of the house may be improved by giving it a unifying coat of paint and removing unwanted ornament and porches that darken the interior.

Drastic changes in the exterior for the sake of making it conform to the current fashion in house design are seldom justified. During the 1920's some old Victorian houses were remodeled to look something like the then popular old English cottage. Ten years later their imitation half-timber, rough stucco walls, and imitation thatched roofs were again out of fashion. A safe rule to follow is to do nothing to the exterior that is not the result of interior changes.

If you follow this rule, the principal changes in the exterior appearance will result from the additional window area that is needed to bring most old houses up to modern needs. Whether you install large sheets of glass in the modern manner or simply add more windows to match the old ones, depends on the condition of the house and your preferences.

In Figure 44, a large farmhouse has been remodeled for the use of a couple whose children have grown up and left home. The one-story wing containing the large kitchen, pantry, and utility room became a large, pleasant living room. Removal of the south porch allows the winter sunshine to enter through the new wide windows. The bedroom and bath have been placed on the first floor, so that the old people need not climb stairs. The kitchen contains automatic laundry equipment to save trips to the basement. The rooms on the second floor may be used as guest rooms, or made into a separate apartment for farm help.

The late Victorian house of Figure 45 was remodeled for a family consisting of parents, three school-age children, and a grandmother who spends the summer months with them. The house lacked closets, the rooms were dark because of the narrow windows, and the kitchen, designed for the hired-girl era, was too remote.

The special needs of the family were a bedroom and bath on the first floor for the grandmother's use, a place for the children's homework and recreation, and a more convenient and central kitchen. The major structural changes were the removal of two chimneys and a bay window. No bearing partitions had to be changed. New wide windows brightened all the rooms. The front bay-window was kept, but new windows were installed to fill the spaces, instead of the awkward narrow windows of the original. The old-fashioned sliding doors were retained between the living room and the combination dining and all-purpose room, because they are often used separately. Between the kitchen and the dining room their extra thickness provided space for a storage wall. A built-in bookcase replaced the sliding door between the hall and the living room.

The useless front porch was converted into a vestibule, and the rest of the space provided closets. The floor of one closet was raised to the level of the stair landing, a change that was made possible by the high ceiling. The back porch, no longer the principal kitchen entrance, is screened and is used as a summer living and dining room. The bedroom made from the old kitchen is oriented away from the porch and the outdoor living area, for privacy and quiet. With an entrance and bathroom close by, it could be used as a rental unit if it were not needed by the family.

EXERCISES

1. Look through old magazines and books for plans of earlier days. List the features that are no longer useful for today's manner of living, such as the icebox in the back entry, service stairways, and the like.

2. If you have a real house as a basis for remodeling, you will need an accurate plan with all windows and doors indicated, and information about the height of the ceilings, the bearing partitions, and location of plumbing and heating pipes. Tentative plans for remodeling may be made by laying a piece of tracing paper over the original plan, and sketching in any possible changes. Use

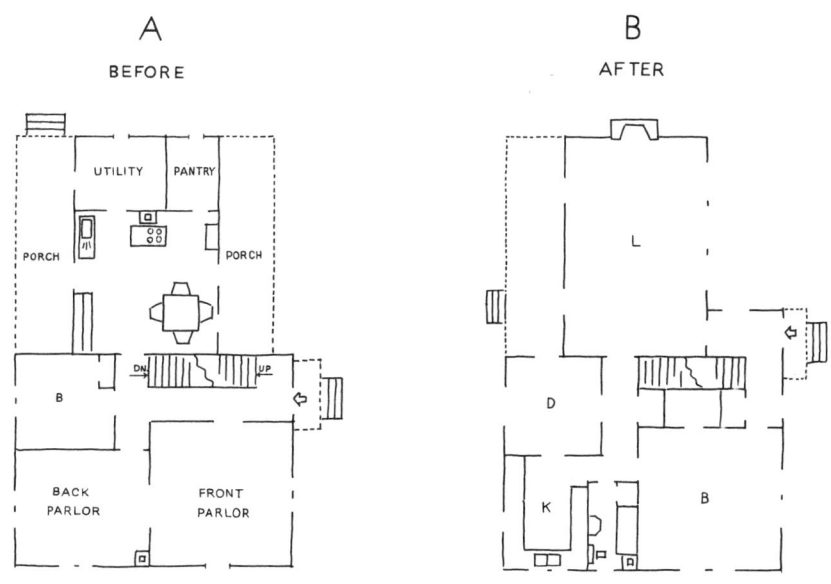

Figure 44

A remodeled farmhouse.

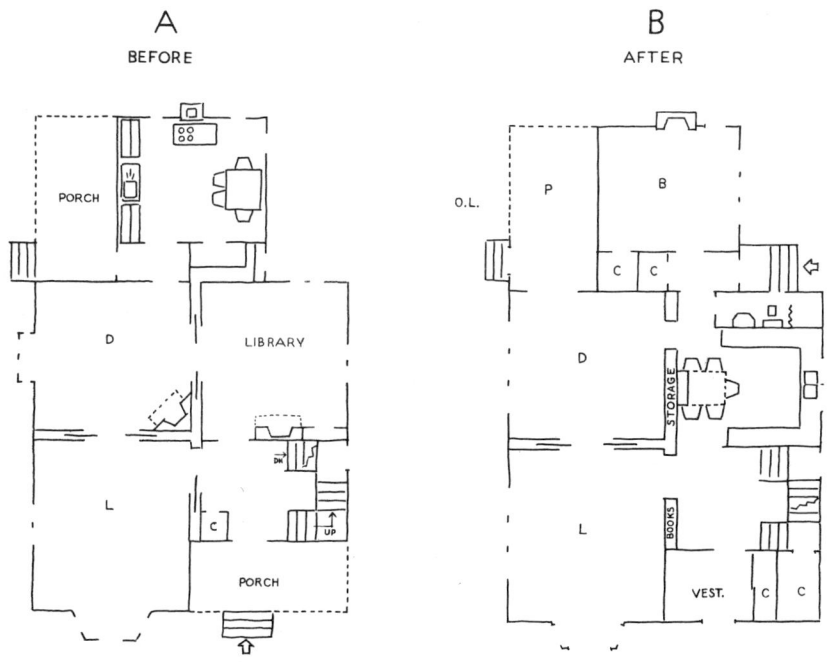

Figure 45

A remodeled Victorian house.

a new sheet of tracing paper for each idea you have on remodeling, so that you may compare them and choose the best. If a bearing partition is to be removed, a ceiling beam will have to take its place.

3. Study the exterior views of houses either in old magazines or use actual houses in your community, and list the features that make it look old-fashioned or poor in design.

4. Study the plans and exterior designs in current magazines, and list the features that you think may be out of date in 10 or 15 years.

READING REFERENCES

Crouse, William H. Home Guide to Repair, Upkeep, and Remodeling. McGraw-Hill Book Company, Inc. New York. 1946.

Frankel, Lee. How to Expand and Improve Your Home. Simmonds-Boardman. New York. 1951.

Hawkins, J. H. Your House, its Upkeep and Rejuvenation. M. Barrows & Company, Inc. New York.

Hawkins, R. R., and C. H. Albee. New Houses from Old. McGraw-Hill Book Company, Inc. New York. 1948.

Tucker, Milton. Buying an Honest House. Little, Brown, & Company. Boston. 1930.

Whitman, Roger. First Aid for the Ailing House. McGraw-Hill Book Company, Inc. New York. 1942.

Chapter XI
An Architect Can Help You

"Art is the butter which enables us to eat the bread
of daily existence without gagging."
                                            Edgell

The simple exercises in drawing floor plans and exteriors in these chapters are not intended to fit you for designing your own house. Such an undertaking is far too difficult and complicated for anyone who has not had special training. Making a few sketches of plans and elevations is in no sense a substitute for that training. These exercises are meant to prepare you to cooperate with an architect, if you decide to build your own house instead of buying a commercially built one.

When the building allowance is limited, you might be tempted to try to get along without the services of an architect, in order to save the cost of his fee. Sooner or later you will discover that this policy is false economy, for a good architect who is experienced in designing small houses contributes the full amount of his fee in the service he gives. He will work out the best possible floor plan for your budget, your lot, and your family, and will help to obtain the best materials and construction for the money available. In addition, he will contribute the beauty of design so conspicuously lacking in most of the houses that come into being without the guidance of an architect. He also draws up forms or proposals and contracts, and generally manages the work of getting ready to build.

If he is employed also to supervise construction, he will visit the house at reasonable intervals, giving his approval for various parts of the work, or withholding it if the terms of the contract have not been complied with. Ordinarily, the specifications call for the written approval of the architect before payments are made by the owner.

Supervision of building by the architect does not mean that he will spend all his time at the house to see that every nail is driven properly. Nor does it mean that he is responsible to the owner for the quality of the contractor's work. The contract lies between the owner and the builder. The architect supervises the latter's work, but he does not guarantee it.

A standard form for a contract between architect and owner has been prepared by the American Institute of Architects, the national professional society. There are many reasons why a written contract between architect and owner is desirable. The average layman is not familiar with the details of architectural practice, and may ask for extra services without realizing it until he receives the bill. If you employ an architect without definite knowledge of what you have a right to expect and what you will have to pay, the way is opened for all sorts of misunderstandings.

Extra payment beyond the usual architect's fee may be asked for an unreasonably large number of preliminary sketches, or changes in plans after the blueprints have been made which necessitate their being redrawn. An architect's fee is generally a certain percentage of the cost of the house for drawing the plans and writing specifications, and a higher percentage if he supervises construction.

As the owner, your duties consist chiefly in giving the architect complete information as to the amount of money you wish to spend, and the size and inclinations of your family. You should also furnish "an accurate survey of the building site, giving the grades and lines of streets, pavements, and adjoining properties; the rights, restrictions, easements, boundaries, and contours of the building site, and full information as to sewer, water, gas, and electric service."*

You also owe it to the architect to make your decisions and return preliminary sketches promptly, just as he owes it to you to finish the plans and specifications within a reasonable time after approval has been given.

In addition, you owe the architect a certain reasonableness of attitude. You must take his word for things. He knows, better than you do, how a house should be built, and how it should look. He knows how much space is needed for various parts of the house, and whether certain ideas of yours are feasible or not. You must not expect him to work financial miracles. Sometimes the plan starts out modestly enough, well within the price limit, but one by one extras are added at the owner's request, until finally the cost is far beyond the original estimate. In such a case you cannot entirely blame the architect. If he is wholly in sympathy with your desires he may not be hard-hearted enough to deny you what you want. He may also suspect that you have not been entirely honest with him about what you can afford, and have a little extra money up your sleeve for these extras you ask for.

Trouble may arise between architect and owner if the contractors' bids are much higher than the architect's estimates. Sharp rises in material and labor costs may occur between the drawing of the plans and figuring of costs by the contractors. Besides, building costs are by their very nature rather nebulous. "...opinions as to the value of a given piece of work may, with entire honesty, vary greatly. If the highest and lowest bidders, with careful working drawings before them differ, as they often do, by 30 or 40 per cent, how can it be wondered at that preliminary estimates made from mere sketches should show wide variations from the lowest bid.

"Therefore, while the architect owes his best efforts to the owner in so important a matter, the owner must in justice forbear hasty judgment if the architect fails to display the gift of divination."**

An architect is usually chosen on the basis of work he has done in the past. Friends who have built recently may recommend him, or examples of his work appearing in magazines may attract your attention. An architect should be selected as carefully as a doctor or a lawyer. Usually a local architect is used, but if one living at a distance is employed, his traveling expenses in connection with his work on the house are paid by the owner.

After you have found an architect who is sympathetic with your desires in the matter of a house, give him complete information as to the amount of money you can spend, the size of your family and its way of life, and your ideas on the kind of house you want.

---

*Day, F. M. *Handbook of Architectural Practice*. American Institute of Architects. Permission to quote granted by the American Institute of Architects, without endorsing or approving the book in which it appears.

**Ibid.

Show him your preliminary sketch plans, but do not expect him to take them over bodily. They are probably full of defects that the untrained eye cannot see, and will have to be put in workable condition. Perhaps the architect will present other ideas much better than your own, and the principal benefit of your own planning will lie in the fact that you can recognize their superiority.

The architect will first make a set of preliminary sketches of plans and exteriors embodying as many of your desires as possible. In the course of a few discussions these preliminary sketches will be worked over and altered until they suit you.

After your approval of the preliminary plans is given, the architect prepares working drawings in exact scale, usually 1/4 inch to 1 foot, showing complete floor plans and elevations of the exterior. When they are accepted, several sets of prints are made from them, for owner, contractor, and architect. Small details of construction and design are also drawn, on a larger scale than that of the floor plans. The placing of the plumbing and heating systems and the electrical wiring are shown on the plan, although some of the details of installation must be left to the special contractors in those fields.

An important part of the architect's work is the writing of building specifications. When you build a house, study the typewritten booklet that accompanies the blueprints as carefully as you study the plans. Specifications consist of exact and detailed instructions as to the materials and methods of construction to be used in the house. The proportions of sand, cement, and gravel for concrete work; the size, species, and grade of lumber for each part of the framing, the brand name of special materials, such as insulation and hardware, and a hundred other details are taken care of in the specifications. These, together with the blueprints, form the main part of the building contract. For that reason their importance can scarcely be overestimated. It would be a good plan to borrow a set of specifications from some friend who has built a house recently, and study them before you embark on your own building venture.

Next, plans and specifications are submitted to building contractors, for bids. A local architect knows the work of the various contractors, and can help select from three to six reliable firms for bidding. Usually, the lowest bid is awarded the contract, although this is not always the best policy. An extremely low bid, much lower than any of the others, may indicate that the contractor intends to make up the difference by skimping on materials or workmanship. In such a case, it would be better to pay more and be certain of good work. The integrity of the contractor is of the utmost importance when you build.

If a general contractor is employed, he will in turn employ sub-contractors for the various types of work, such as masonry, carpentry, and plastering. If you are able to give a great deal of time and attention to the building of the house, and if you know a great deal about construction, you may prefer to do the work of the general contractor himself, and deal directly with the subcontractors. Such a policy is scarcely practicable for the average person who has a full-time job of his own.

After the building contract has been signed, construction work usually begins promptly and should continue rapidly until the house is finished, for it is to your advantage to take possession as soon as possible. Usually the contract specifies a definite date for the completion of the house, so that the contractor or the workmen will not be tempted to spend part of their time on other jobs that may turn up.

A large, well-organized construction company can build a number of houses at one time without delay, but in the country and in small towns building organizations are less tightly knit. If you do not have a time limit in the contract, you may find your house at a standstill because the workers have taken a few days off to do a little remodeling job for someone else.

If it is necessary to make changes in either the plans or the materials after building operations have started, such changes should be authorized by the architect in writing. The owner should not give verbal orders for changes to the contractor or the workmen, unless he is prepared to pay handsomely for them.

Chapter XII
Historic Design in Houses

"It is well to have as many holds upon happiness as possible."
                                                                Jane Austen

Part 1
European Styles

Modern design in houses has developed in this country quite recently, but it has come to be so generally accepted that we almost forget how much we used to be dominated by traditional ideas in architectural design. As late as 1930, many people cared a great deal about building an "authentic" house, that is, one whose design had been copied faithfully in every detail from some period of the past.

The design of large buildings also was borrowed from the past in those days. Churches had to be Gothic, or Romanesque, or Renaissance. Bank buildings and post offices were often classical, and the early skyscrapers were dressed up with either classical or Gothic details that had nothing to do with their steel frame structures. Compare the Woolworth building in New York, or the Tribune building in Chicago, with the United Nations building in New York, to see how completely modern design has turned away from copying the past.

The historic styles are still worth studying, however, even though we do not intend to copy them. Architecture is one of the arts--an important part of our cultural heritage. And the enjoyment of the arts furnishes one of the paths we may follow in the pursuit of happiness mentioned in the Declaration of Independence.

Even if you plan to build a modern house that will in no way resemble any house of the past, it will be worth your while to learn something of the historic background of house design. You will gain a deeper understanding of the world you live in, as well as a new source of interest and enjoyment.

Travel will mean more to you, for wherever you go, in this country and in Europe, you will find beautiful old houses, many of which are open to the public. The restorations at Williamsburg, the famous old houses of Natchez, and the colonial houses of New England, all draw thousands of visitors from all over the country. The more you know, the more you will see, when you visit such places. In every age and every country there have been some people who have lavished time and money on their houses, in the belief that they were more than shelter, that houses could be works of art. The results of their labors are yours to look at and enjoy.

Traditional house design, as we find it in this country, has been borrowed mainly from England and western Europe. Regardless of the country of origin, such houses may be divided roughly into two kinds of design, the classical, or formal, and the medieval, or picturesque. In terms of architecture, the word "classical" refers to the designs of ancient Greece and Rome, and their later revival and adaptation during the Renaissance. The picturesque styles are generally based on the houses that were built during the Middle Ages, both large mansions and the unpretentious peasant cottages of the countryside.

The great marble temples of the Acropolis at Athens provide an example of the basic forms of Classical architecture. The Parthenon, built during the Fifth Century, B. C., is the best-known Greek temple. The principal variations in Greek design are the Doric, the Ionic, and the Corinthian, which is related to Ionic. Regular space divisions and formal balance are characteristic of Greek architecture. In spite of the vertical lines of the columns, the heavy entablature and the flattened gable roof of the Greek temple produce a dominant horizontal feeling.

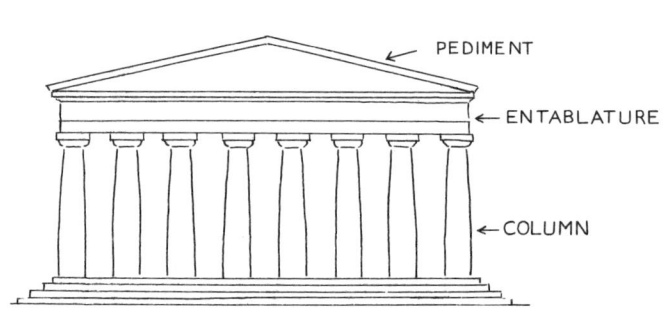

Figure 46

A Greek temple.

The Romans borrowed and adapted Greek design; they developed the arch, which permitted wider openings in walls, as well as curving structures, such as vaulted roofs, and domes. While many Roman temples were patterned directly on the Greek models, some were circular, covered by a dome. The Pantheon in Rome, built during the Second Century A. D., is a circular structure with an impressive dome. The entrance portico of the Pantheon repeats the form of the front of a Greek temple.

The dwellings of the ancient world have had little influence on the houses of America, but we shall see the temple form, the arch, and even the dome, in the houses of the 18th and 19th centuries.

The architectural designs of ancient Rome were carried to all parts of the Empire; in the eastern Mediterranean area, under oriental influence, they developed into what is called the Byzantine style. After the fall of Rome, western Europe was for several centuries in a state of chaos. A new, Christian, civilization slowly developed, called the Medieval period, or the Middle Ages. Early medieval architecture is called Romanesque. It is solid and heavy, with round arches, rather small openings, and vaulted roofs.

During the Medieval period Romanesque architecture in turn developed into new forms, called Gothic, beginning in northern France, and spreading through western Europe and England. Gothic architecture has given us the great cathedrals of northern Europe, as well as many secular buildings. Gothic cathedrals are essentially vertical in feeling; horizontal lines are subordinated, while soaring towers and spires lift the eye upward. Less attention was paid to formal balance and regular spacing than in classical architecture.

Carvings of human figures and other natural forms were used in a spontaneous, free spirit. Characteristic details of Gothic cathedrals are pointed arches, rose windows, buttresses, fan vaulting, and spires. In the interior the great height is enhanced by the vertical lines of clustered pillars and ribbed vaulting. The beauti-

Figure 47
A half-timber house of medieval England.

Figure 48
A Cotswold house of stone.

ful colored glass windows of cathedrals such as Chartres form one of the most impressive sights that American tourists can see on their travels abroad.

As to the dwellings of the middle ages, the center of early feudal life was at first the castle, which served for both dwelling and fortress. Later, as times became more settled, small houses in towns and country developed into forms that have set the pattern for what is called romantic or picturesque house design.

The cottages of medieval England have been the principal source of ideas for picturesque houses in this country. In general shape they were irregular, with broken roof lines and an informally balanced arrangement of windows and doors. Often the upper story projected beyond the wall beneath. A vertical feeling was given to the medieval house by its steeply pitched roof, the gables, and the tall numerous chimneys. Leaded casement windows were used, singly, or in groups, according to the size and importance of the room within. "Leaded" means small panes of glass, either rectangular or diamond-shaped, set in narrow strips of lead.

Medieval builders had to use whatever materials could be found locally, since transportation facilities were limited. Early roofs were of thatch (overlapping layers of straw built up to a thickness of a foot or more). Later, tile and slate were generally used to cover roofs.

The walls were built on a framework of massive timbers, the spaces between them filled in with brick. Often the bricks were covered with stucco, producing the pattern of dark and light stripes that is called "half-timber". This method of building walls was used in northern Europe as well as in England. By the beginning of the 17th century timber was getting scarce, and solid brick walls soon became the standard. The new fashion for Renaissance design was also coming in at that time.

Applied decoration of the medieval English house consisted of carving on the timbers, and sometimes moulded designs in the stucco, called pargetting. The principal decoration, however, was inherent in the materials themselves; the dark and light pattern of the half-timber, and the varied surfaces of stone, slate, and handmade brick. Richly textured materials such as these need no added ornament.

Houses were built entirely of stone in those regions where it was plentiful. The Cotswold district is famous for its beautiful stone houses. In their steep roofs and gables, large chimneys, and small casement windows, Cotswold houses resemble the other medieval English houses.

In a way, it is a mistake to use the word "style" in speaking of medieval houses. Their builders were not aware that they were creating a picturesque style of architecture that would be copied centuries later. They were simply building the best kind of shelter possible with the materials and technical skill at their command. Their houses are handsome because of their fitness to site and materials, their honesty of design, and also because men had artistic talent and the ability to create beauty then just as they have now.

At three different times the houses of medieval England have influenced the design of American houses. The first time was in the 17th century, when the Pilgrims, quite naturally, built their houses in the new world after the pattern of their childhood homes in England. The second occasion was during the 19th century, when Victorian Gothic houses repeated some of the features of the medieval house, somewhat scrambled together with scroll-saw ornament, bracketed porches, and cupolas. The third time was during the 1920's, when Tudor houses were copied faithfully and with great enthusiasm all over the country.

Following the Middle Ages, the Renaissance brought to western Europe a return of interest in Classical architecture. The new style developed first in Italy, and gradually spread northward through Europe, arriving finally in England. As opposed to Gothic design, Renaissance structures displayed formal balance and regular space divisions, in both the arrangement of masses and the disposition of windows and doors. Ornament was subordinated to structure. A strong horizontal feeling was enhanced by entablatures and cornices. The round arch replaced the pointed arch. Pediments, columns, pilasters, and other details borrowed from classical sources were used as decorations. Large domes were used on many churches. St. Peter's in Rome is the most famous of these domed buildings.

English architecture began to show the influence of the Italian Renaissance during the 16th century, the change beginning with palaces and large mansions, and gradually extending to the small house. Henry VIII had tried to introduce the Renaissance style into England, but its nature was imperfectly understood at that time by the English builder, who mixed Classic and Gothic details in an awkward fashion.

The new style was firmly established in England during the 17th century, when Sir Christopher Wren, the most famous architect England has produced, favored it in his design for St. Paul's cathedral and the many small churches that had to be rebuilt after the great fire of London in 1666.

St. Paul's cathedral is another famous domed structure. The smaller English Renaissance church was of Greek-temple form, with a pillared portico, and a tower somewhat in the form of a telescope, with stories of diminishing size ornamented with Classical details. We still call them "Christopher Wren" towers, for their designer. They were used on secular buildings as well as churches.

Many of the public buildings in this country are of Renaissance design. Our national capitol is another famous domed structure, and many of the state capitols

Figure 49

An Italian Renaissance palace.

Figure 50

A house of the English Renaissance.

also have domes and Greek-temple porticos. Independence Hall in Philadelphia has a Christopher Wren tower.

Italian Renaissance palaces furnished the pattern for the design of the great English mansions that were built during the 17th and 18th centuries. These, in turn, were copied in the building of smaller houses. The new style called for definite changes in design. The old freedom of arrangement that went with the informal design of the medieval house was replaced by strict formal balance. Sometimes the convenience of the interior was sacrificed for the symmetry demanded of the exterior.

"The gulf between the Renaissance and Gothic building is deep and fundamental. The Gothic house was mainly the product of simple contemporary requirements; based on a rough preliminary plan, perhaps scratched on stone by the master mason, the conception was altered ... as the work progressed. The Renaissance house was entirely the product of one man's mind and was fully designed, both in plan and elevation, before the work was begun."*

The typical small Renaissance house of England was of a two-story rectangular shape, built of brick. The gable or hip roof was finished at the edge with mouldings in the style of a classical cornice. Since the Greek temple was the ideal of Renaissance design, it was natural that roofs should become flatter as the style developed.

The doorway, in the exact center of the facade, was the dominant feature of the design. It was flanked by columns surmounted by entablature and pediment, which gave it the name "temple-front" doorway. Large double-hung windows were arranged on either side of the doorway in formal balance, with regularly repeated space divisions. Houses of this type continued to stay in fashion during the 18th century and on into the 19th, with only minor changes. They are often called "Georgian" houses, for the kings who ruled England during that time.

The term "Regency" is often applied to English houses of the early 19th century. Historically, the Regency was the decade from 1810 to 1820, when George IV

---

*Dutton, Ralph. *The English Country House*. Charles Scribner's Sons. New York. 1936.

served as regent for his demented father. In the matter of architecture and decoration, however, the term is more loosely interpreted and covers a longer period of time. Regency designers turned directly to ancient Greece and Rome for their ideas, instead of using designs filtered through Italian Renaissance usage.

In their general character, Regency houses were similar to those of the earlier Georgian period; that is, formal balance was used, and ornament, where it was employed, was mostly of classical origin. Details were simpler and larger in scale than formerly. The general tendency through the later Georgian period was toward flatter roofs and larger windows. Often the wall was extended up above the edge of the roof to form a coping, and gave the appearance, from the ground, of an entirely flat roof.

An interest in Chinese design had persisted in England ever since the development, during the 17th century, of trade with the Orient. This interest was expressed mainly in furniture and fabric design, but during the Regency period it appeared in the pagoda-shaped hoods used over doorways and bay windows that replaced the Classical doorway of the earlier Georgian period.

The smaller Georgian house has furnished the pattern for many American houses, both during the colonial period and in the present, as well as the recent past. The Regency style has also been used in this country to some extent. Its flattened roof, large windows, and simple design make it somewhat akin to modern architecture. Adaptations of Regency, sometimes called "classic modern" are also used.

In other European countries, the change from medieval to Renaissance house design was similar to that in England. Random arrangement gave way to formal balance and orderly spacing. Windows became larger, and medieval ornament was replaced by details borrowed from Classical sources.

French houses, especially the smaller country houses, showed a wide variety of design according to location. In the northern section, medieval houses resembled those of England, with steep roofs, half-timber walls, and small-paned casement windows. In the south, the houses looked more like those of Spain and Italy, with flatter roofs and walls of stone or stucco. German and Swiss influence appeared in the eastern sections of France.

Figure 51

A French Chateau.

The development of French architecture may be traced in the design of the great chateaux. The earliest of them were heavy solid fortresses with battlements and towers. Later, there was a long transitional period when Renaissance details were added to the irregular shape, steep hip roof, towers, and elaborate dormers of the Gothic style. The steeply pitched roof remained through the Renaissance as a feature of French buildings, although formal balance, regular arrangement, emphasis on the horizontal, and classical details brought them closer to the Italian style.

The influence of French design on colonial American may be seen in New Orleans and other cities settled by the French. Later, during the Victorial period and on into the early 20th century, the famous chateaux of France served as models for the houses of wealthy Americans. The show place of many towns was a mansion with a steep mansard roof, towers, and elaborate dormer windows. "Biltmore" in North Carolina, which is now open to the public, is one of the most famous of these houses.

During the 1920's, when American interest in picturesque houses was strong, the medieval cottages of northern France shared the popularity of the old English house. In many houses built at that time, features of both English and Norman were combined.

Part 2
Colonial Houses

The term "colonial" is generally used for the period between the coming of the first settlers to New England in the early 17th century, and the end of the war for independence, in 1780. This period is so long and saw so many changes, that it is convenient to divide it into two major parts, with the division point about 1700. The first part is often called "Pilgrim", or Early Colonial, while the second is called "Georgian", or Late Colonial, to indicate the influence of 18th century Englist architecture on the houses of the colonies.

The climate, the local resources, and the social background of the settlers all had an influence on the design of houses. In the northern colonies compact plans, low ceilings, and smaller windows helped to keep the house warm during the long winters. In the south, higher ceilings, two-story porches, larger windows, and spacious rooms contributed to comfort in hot weather and also furnished a setting for the more liberal social life of the southern colonists.

Many minor variations may be found in the houses of the different colonies, and even in different sections of the same colony. In the early days, especially, the building of a house was a local enterprise. What plans there were had to be drawn by the owner, since there were no professional architects. The lack of transportation forced the use of local materials, and labor was furnished by relatives and neighbors. It was natural, then, that houses in a given locality should have a family resemblance, sometimes quite different from the houses in the next town.

Variations according to time were much more pronounced than those produced by location. For one thing, the definite style change from Gothic to Renaissance took place in England during the colonial period, and before long reached across the ocean to influence American houses. At the same time, conditions of living in the new world underwent a change. From 1620 to 1700 the wilderness was subdued and towns were established. The houses built during the earlier years reflect in their design the primitive and arduous life of their builders; the later colonial houses show the prosperity and luxury of a flourishing society.

Seventeenth century colonial houses resembled the medieval English house. At the time the Pilgrims were establishing their settlements in New England, the influence of the Italian Renaissance was beginning to show in England, but the Pilgrims carried with them the memory of the older houses in which they had lived as children. The first houses they built, then, were Gothic in character, with steep roofs, an overhang of the upper stories, and small-paned casement windows.

Figure 52

An early New England Colonial house.

The main difference between Pilgrim houses and those of the old country was the use of shingles or siding to cover the outside walls, instead of the exposed pattern of half-timber work. This difference was, at least in the earlier houses, only on the surface. Under the shingle covering of some of these houses, typical half-timber construction has been found. No doubt the older form of building proved inadequate for the bitter winters of the new country and had to be covered with wood as an added protection from the cold.

The typical Pilgrim house was bare of applied decoration. The lack of ornament is not to be wondered at if one considers the hardships of early colonial life. Ornament of any kind indicates leisure, and one is safe in assuming that nobody had much spare time in those days. The austere religious beliefs of the Pilgrims, also, must have been barren soil for the cultivation of the arts.

Trees were plentiful everywhere; consequently, most of the early houses were built of wood. The granite of New England was too hard to be worked with the crude tools of the day. In sections where the softer limestone was found, however, it was used for building. Travelers through Pennsylvania and lower New York still enjoy the stout dignified stone colonial houses, and their equally handsome stone barns. In parts of the southern colonies, heat and dampness shortened the life of wood structures, and led to the early use of brick for building.

During the entire colonial period, England set the fashions for the American colonies. Clothing, furniture, and houses were patterned after the styles of the mother country. We have seen that the earliest colonial houses resembled those of medieval England. When that style gave way to Renaissance design, American houses soon followed the English example.

In England the spread of the classic style was accompanied during the 18th century by a popular interest in architecture and decoration. It became the fashionable thing to know something of these subjects. Many wealthy amateurs designed their own houses. Books on the new style were published in England and soon found their way across the ocean. In the new country they were studied and copied by Colonial builders.

Figure 53

A Georgian Colonial Mansion.

Colonial houses of the 18th century, then, were patterned after houses of Georgian England. In general shape they were solidly rectangular and formally balanced, like their English models. Roofs became flatter, and were finished at the edge with a classical cornice. The doorway was the center of interest, with the same temple-front decoration that was used in England. Large double-hung windows were formally balanced and evenly spaced. The details of doorways, roof cornices, and windows were usually based on designs found in the books mentioned above.

The very small houses of both the early and later colonial periods were simple one-story or story-and-a-half cottages, with small-paned windows, shutters, and little ornament at the doorway. The "Cape Cod" cottage that was so popular during the 20's and 30's was copied from the small colonial house. (See Figure 38).

In Florida and California, the early Spanish settlers left their mark on building tradition, to be seen today in the old ranch houses and the missions. During the 1920's, the love of picturesque houses that led to the use of old English and Norman designs in the east was expressed, in Florida and the western states, by romantic Spanish houses. You can still see them in the older residential sections, with their red tile roofs, rough stucco walls, and wrought iron grills. Actually, Spanish and Italian provincial designs were often used together in the same house, leading to the use of the term "Mediterranean" to describe them.

One important feature of the original Mediterranean house, the arrangement of rooms about a central court, has carried over into the present day, because it fits in so well with our ideas on outdoor living. Such an arrangement is well adapted to hot climates, especially in towns, where an enclosed space open to the sky provides a place where the family may enjoy cool evenings without the sacrifice of privacy.

The Colonial period, historically speaking, came to an end with the winning of the war for independence. In house design, the influence of the Renaissance continued, with slight changes, beyond the end of the century. The term "Federal" has come into use to describe the houses that were built in the latter years of the 18th century. There is no real dividing line between the "Georgian Colonial" and the "Federal" styles. Usually the term Federal is used for the tall, square, flat-roofed three-story town houses built by the wealthier citizens of the young Republic.

The details were classical in character, but somewhat simpler, and larger in scale than in the earlier houses. Formal balance and strict regularity in the arrangement of windows continued to be followed. The name of Samuel McIntire is associated with some of the finest Federal houses. Born in 1759, he worked as master builder, designer, and wood carver. The Pierce-Nichols house and the Pingree house, in Salem, Mass., which he built, are now open to the public.

The Greek Revival period began in the early years of the 19th century, introducing a new interpretation of classic architecture. It is true that the Georgian colonial house, with its temple-front doorway was of Greek origin. It had come to America by a round-about route, through the Italian renaissance, and then through the English Georgian style In Renaissance design, Greek details were used in miniature, so to speak, as decoration applied to the surface of the house, rather than as parts of the structure.

Figure 54

A Federal Mansion.

The Greek Revival house was different, in that its entire form was patterned after the Greek temple. It was turned end-wise to the street, with a two-story portico in the form of a Greek temple across the front. Two-story porticos had been used in the Georgian colonial period, especially in the southern colonies, but they came out at right angles to the main line of the roof, while the portico of the Greek Revival house was an extension of the main roof. "The distinctive characteristic of the classic Revival ... a pediment carrying through and roofing the building without breaks ... The pediment had heretofore been independent of the roof and abutted against it, the building being invariably wider than the portico."*

Figure 55

A Greek Revival house.

The Greek Revival style ended about the middle of the 19th century. The Victorian period, which followed, was one of great variety in house design. Books and magazines of the time show pictures of houses that were supposed to be copies of medieval fortresses, half-timber cottages, Swiss chalets, Italian villas, and French chateaux. Most of them were not very good copies, at that.

Generally speaking, Victorian houses were of a romantic, picturesque type of design, with informal balance, broken lines, and irregular masses. Towers,

---

*Major, Howard. *Domestic Architecture of the Early American Republic*. J. B. Lippincott Company. Philadelphia. 1926.

porches, balconies, bay windows, gables, and dormers were used freely. High ceilings, tall narrow windows, high chimneys, and towers made the Victorian house essentially vertical in feeling, as opposed to the horizontal dominance of Greek Revival and Georgian houses.

Figure 56

A Victorian house with a mansard roof.

As the period progressed, ornament seemed to become more important than the structural character of the house itself. The rapid expansion of the country, together with industrial development, put wealth in the hands of many people who lacked cultural background, whose taste had not been developed by education, travel, and other advantages.* The Horatio Alger theme of a ragged orphan who, by thrift and diligence, becomes a rich man, occurred many times in real life, all over the country. An undeveloped taste is likely to mistake lavish ornament for beauty. It takes study and training to appreciate the quieter and less obvious beauty that lies in order, proportion and simple honest structure.

Toward the end of the 19th century a reaction set in against the ornate Victorian house, especially against the use of gingerbread ornament and the indiscriminate mixing of historic designs. Two influences can be seen developing during this time. One was strongly traditional, based on careful study and copying of historic design, especially that of the Renaissance.

The other influence, foreshadowing the coming of modern design, expressed a complete departure from historic styles. The early houses of Frank Lloyd Wright, in and near Chicago, are the best-known examples of this influence. They were the direct opposite of the tall ornate Victorian house. They were low and wide, with flattened roofs that extended far beyond the walls, and groups of rather small casement windows. They have been called "prairie houses" because they dramatized

---

*"'Before we left Atlanta I was dickering for that big lot on Peachtree...'
'Oh, Rhett, how lovely! I do so want a house of my own. A great big one...I know just what I want. It's the newest thing ... It was modeled after a Swiss chalet... It was lovely. It had a high mansard roof with a picket fence on the top and a tower made of fancy shingles at each end. And the towers had windows with red and blue glass in them. It was so stylish looking.'
'I suppose it had jigsaw work on the porch banisters...and a fringe of wood scrollwork hanging from the roof of the porch?'
'Yes.'
'Why not a Creole house or a Colonial with six white columns?'
'I tell you I don't want anything tacky and old-fashioned looking.'"**

**Mitchell, Margaret. Gone With the Wind. The Macmillan Company. New York. 1937.

the horizontal lines of the land in the middle west. According to Lewis Mumford, the design of these houses was "vulgarized in the Craftsman bungalow and later in the ranch house".*

The development of the bungalow (often called the California bungalow) is also credited to the Greene brothers, architects whose houses, built in California about the turn of the century, were notable examples of careful craftsmanship in wood.**

For the first decade or so of the 20th century the bungalow was a popular design for small houses. In a way it was a new form of house design, for it was not copied from historic styles. Where the Victorian house had been tall and narrow and loaded with ornament, the bungalow was low and broad and bare of applied decoration.

The main idea of craftsman bungalow design was that the construction of the house, such as the shaping and fitting together of beams and rafters, was in itself decorative, and should not be covered. Any kind of applied ornament, either jigsaw gingerbread or classical columns and cornices, was considered dishonest, because it was not a part of the structure.

Honesty of design was supposed to be shown in the bungalow by exposed rafter ends and ceiling beams. (In actual practice, economy sometimes forced the use of imitations; ceiling beams were thin strips of wood nailed to the plaster, and the effect of wide rafters was gained by fastening short little boards to the under side of the overhang.) Brackets were sometimes used under the wide overhang, but they were heavy and structural-looking, not at all like the jigsaw brackets of the Victorian house. It might be said also that these brackets were not really needed to hold up the roof.

Figure 57

A bungalow of the early 20th century.

The horizontal effect of the bungalow was enhanced by the wide roof and by heavy boards defining the upper and lower edges of groups of rather small windows. The windows were often set rather high in the wall, so that stout oak bookcases and buffets could be built in under them. That was the day of window-seats, Morris chairs, and mission furniture in fumed oak. Massive cobblestone or brick fireplaces, often extending up to the ceiling, were a feature of bungalow living rooms. On the exterior, heavy stone or brick porch pillars emphasized the low, solid, and somewhat rustic character of the house.

---

*New Yorker. Nov. 28, 1953.
**Architectural Forum. September 1948.

HISTORIC DESIGN IN HOUSES

Figure 58

A bungalow interior.

A short lull in home building during the first world war was followed by about a decade of intense interest in historic styles. The Craftsman bungalow went out of fashion. The colonial styles, and the small provincial houses of medieval Europe, were especially liked. Anyone who remembers the swarms of American tourists who swept through Europe every summer during the 1920's can easily understand why the European house designs became so popular.

Americans were seeing for the first time the picturesque and quaint old cottages of England and France, and the charming and picturesque old hillside houses of Italy and Spain. They were a new and enchanting sight. Many Americans were planning to build at that time, and it was perhaps natural that they should try to recapture in their new houses the qualities of quaintness and charm that had delighted their eyes on their trip abroad.

Old numbers of magazines devoted to houses will give you a picture of the interests of their readers during the 1920's. Articles on old English, French, Spanish, and Italian houses filled their pages, along with pictures and descriptions of the copies of them that had been built in this country. The ethical problems involved in the use of imitation half-timber and thatching were gravely discussed, and helpful hints were given on how to build a convincing effect of a sagging roof.

The captions and descriptions that went with the pictures reveal the romantic attitude toward house design that prevailed in those days. The words "Quaint",. "picturesque", and "charming" occurred frequently.* There were titles such as "A bit of Old France in the Heart of New England", and "The Authentic English (or Spanish or French or Italian) House." "Authentic" meant that every detail had been copied faithfully from some period, not necessarily from the same house, but gathered together from houses of the same type.

The copying of old houses sometimes developed into copying the effects of age, such as the sagging roof-line mentioned above. Beams and boards were cut and hacked to look old and warped; brick and stucco were mingled with irregular edges to suggest crumbling walls. When a brick wall was painted white, the paint was carefully wiped off a few bricks here and there, to make it look old and weathered.

Generally speaking, the English and French styles were most popular in the east and the middle west, and the Mediterranean styles were used most in the far west. But if you look through the old magazines you will find quaint old English cottages with palm trees and cactus in the front yard, and also Italian farmhouses nestling picturesquely in the foothills of the Berkshires.

---

*In recent years the favorite words have been "dramatic" and "exciting", but "elegant" is catching up with them.

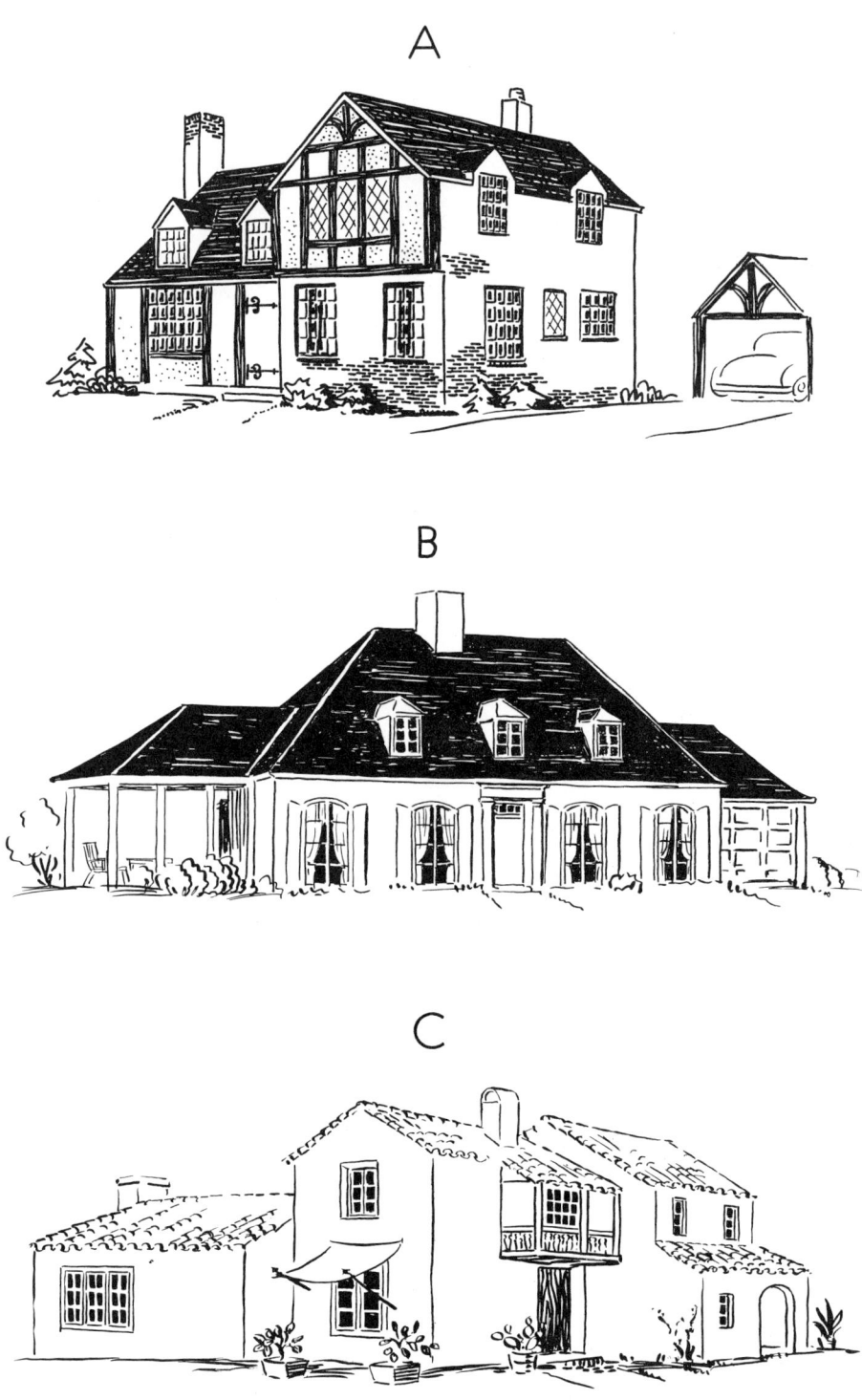

Figure 59

English, French, and Spanish houses were copied during the 1920's.

Hardware manufacturers produced a special line of antique-style door hinges and latches so that the quaint effect of the house need not be marred by any details that were reminders of the machine age. Light fixtures were designed to look like primitive candle-holders, and even the electric door-bell was dressed up with a wrought-iron escutcheon of antique design. In spite of this intense interest in the effect of age on the outside, nobody seemed to mind the motor car in the garage, or the plumbing, wiring, and modern heating system within the house.

Rather unsatisfactory plans often went with those quaint old-style exteriors. A great deal of space was used in hallways. The picturesque effects of gables and dormers were often paid for with bedrooms that were poorly lighted and ventilated, or of such irregular shape that the arrangement of furniture was a problem.

In the descriptions that accompanied the pictures of a new house there were frequent allusions to the "effect" of the gable or the doorway, or some other outside feature, but relatively little was said about the interior with reference to what it was like to live in. Sunny rooms in winter, summer breezes, pleasant views from the windows, and privacy for outdoor living were not often emphasized. You would almost think that houses existed for the purpose of being looked at from the outside, rather than of being lived in on the inside.

The house designs of colonial America shared in the popularity of traditional styles. There were also magazine articles entitled "The Authentic Colonial House", with pictures of the proper kinds of windows, doors, and other details. The 18th century form of colonial house was most frequently copied, although the earlier 17th century houses were also used, especially by collectors of antique furniture. Smaller houses were patterned after the one-story colonial cottage, usually called the Cape Cod house.

Several influences were soon to change the course of American house design. The depression that began in 1929 brought home building to a standstill for a time. When building began again the construction of a house was a matter for strict economy. Home builders were concerned with getting as much living space for their limited funds as possible. The picturesque styles were abandoned, for they were not economical; such features as broken roof lines and half-timber (even the imitation) cost extra, and now the extra money was not at hand.

The simpler colonial styles became more popular following the depression, largely because they offered the most house for the money. Their plain rectangular shape, simple roof, and uncomplicated plan were economical, as was stock millwork in colonial design. The Cape Cod cottage was especially popular at this time, for it contained a surprising amount of space within its compact story-and-a-half shape.

Another influence was at work during the 1930's. The modern movement in architecture, interrupted earlier in the century by the revival of traditionalism, now became stronger. This movement was partly a rebellion against the slavish copying of historic styles. Its principal motive, however, was an earnest attempt to make a new approach to the problems of the house with regard to modern materials and techniques, as well as modern ways of living.

Since this new movement was much more than just a new fashion in exterior appearance, the modern house must be spoken of first in terms of its interior space as it developed in response to the demands of contemporary life. Some of the features of today's way of living, as they have influenced the house, are:

1. Higher building costs have forced down the size of houses. As rooms have become fewer in number and smaller, the ceilings lower, an open plan, with rooms over-lapping or only partly divided, has been used to give an illusion of space. In many cases finished ceilings have been omitted, and the roof itself, with exposed rafters, has taken its place.

2. The disappearance of domestic servants has also helped to produce the open plan. Most of the older ideas on house planning were derived from the rather formal upper-class way of life of past centuries. For instance, it used to be considered necessary to have a pantry between the kitchen and the dining room so that the noise made by the servants in the kitchen might not be heard by the family and their guests at the table.

Today the kitchen work is usually done by the lady of the house herself, with the collaboration of the family, and often of the guests, too. There is no reason for setting the kitchen apart. In many modern houses it is merely an extension of the living area, with only a token partition in the form of a cupboard or a counter to hide the disorder incidental to cooking.

Figure 60

Room spaces overlap in an open plan.

The hired girl has been replaced by electrical equipment that has taken away much of the drudgery of housekeeping. With its help any intelligent woman can do her own work and still find time for the gracious living mentioned in magazine advertising, or for employment outside her home.

3. Everyday use of the motor car demands that the garage be readily accessible from both the house and the street. Alleys are seldom used in modern subdivisions, because of their cost. The front garage has become a sort of symbol of modern house design. Compare a stately Georgian colonial house, with its symmetrical arrangement of the parlor windows, and its classical doorway, with a modern house that has garage, kitchen, and other service features on the street side. The older house presents a façade whose design seems to exist for its own sake, while the new house is a casual expression of the plan within. In fact, "facade" is much too dressy a word for the unimpressive street side of many modern houses.

4. Interest in outdoor living has influenced the design of the house. If you also compare the rear views of the colonial house and the modern one,

you would probably find the kitchen door, back porch, and other service features, with little attention to architectural enrichment, on the first; at the back door of the modern house you will find a handsome terrace and large windows that afford a view of the garden to the principal rooms. In other words, the modern house has reversed its position, and presents its most important side to the back.

5. Another feature of modern life is a generally faster pace. We are too busy or too impatient to take care of elaborate or delicate furnishings. A typical modern remark about the detailed carving of colonial woodwork is, "I'd hate to have to dust that." Modern interiors are characterized by an absence of detail, and surfaces of plywood, brick, or stone that either do not show the dirt or can be cleaned quickly with mechanical tools.

Modern houses vary so much in their exterior appearance that they are hard to describe. They have a few features in common. They are not copied from traditional design, the exterior develops from the use of space within, large glass areas are used for the principal rooms, and usually they have horizontal, rather than a vertical feeling.

The term "International" is often applied to one type of modern house that originated in Europe. It is a house that consists of severe rectangular forms, with smooth white walls, a flat roof, and continuous horizontal strips of windows.

Another type of house might be called "rustic modern". It features the use of brick or rough stone for both interior and exterior walls, combined with dark-stained wood. Many of these houses have wide low roofs, with exposed rafters, and resemble the old craftsman bungalow.

Experiments in new materials and techniques of building have produced a variety of exterior designs in modern houses. Igloo and mushroom shapes, made by spraying concrete on huge balloons, triangular and spiral forms, all-glass houses, and many others, have appeared in recent years. Some modern houses stand up above ground on stilts, others are cantilivered out far beyond their foundations, and still others are half-buried in the side of a hill.

For the general public, the most popular house of the decade following the second world war has been the commercially-built "ranch-style" house. It is a low, spread-out one-story house, with a flattened roof, usually with a wide over-

Figure 61

Many ranch-style houses of today resemble bungalows.

Figure 62

A modern hillside house.

Figure 63

A hillside house on stilts.

hang. Materials are wood, brick, and stone, and often a combination of all three in the same house. Doorways of ranch-style houses are non-traditional in design, and windows are often casement or awning type, except for the picture window, a wide sheet of fixed glass flanked by two smaller windows. Some of the more conservative builders try to compromise with the past, and build what might be called colonial ranch houses, with gray or white siding, small-paned windows, green shutters, and a demure pediment over the front door.

EXERCISES

1. Visit the newer residential districts in your town. Note the ways in which the houses differ from those in the older sections.

2. If you live in a part of the country where old houses are open to the public, visit them and study their interior arrangement in terms of living today.

3. If you have access to bound volumes of architectural magazines, trace the development of the modern house. Note the architects whose names are connected with the outstanding houses.

READING REFERENCES

European Houses

Addy, Sidney O. The Evolution of the English House. George Allen & Unwin, Ltd. London. 1933.
Batsford, Harry, and Charles Fry. The English Cottage. B. T. Batsford, Ltd. London. 1938.
Braun, Hugh. The Story of the English House. Charles Scribner's Sons. New York. 1940.
Chamberlain, Samuel. Through France with a Sketchbook. Robert M. McBride & Company. New York. 1929.
Dutton, Ralph. The English Country House. Charles Scribner's Sons. New York. 1936.

Churchill, Randolph. *Fifteen Famous English Homes*. Verschoyle. London. 1954.
Eberlein, H. D. *Villas of Florence and Tuscany*. J. B. Lippincott Company. Philadelphia. 1922.
Lloyd, Nathaniel. *A History of the English House*. William Hellburn. New York. 1931.
Newcomb, Rexford. *The Spanish House for America*. J. B. Lippincott Company. Philadelphia. 1927.
Richardson, A. E., and H. D. Eberlein. *The Smaller English House of the Later Renaissance*. William Hellburn. New York. 1925.
Summerson, John. *Architecture in Britain*, 1530-1830. Penguin Books, Inc. Baltimore. 1958.
Tallmadge, T. F. *The Story of England's Architecture*. W. W. Norton & Company, Inc. New York. 1934.
The Connoisseur. *Period Guides to the Houses, Decoration, Furniture and Chattels of the Classic Periods*. 6 volumes. Reynal & Co. New York. 1958.
Turnor, Reginald. *The Smaller English House, 1500 - 1939*.
Whiteman, G. W. *Some Famous English Country Homes*. Antique Collector, Ltd. London. 1953.

American Houses

Chamberlain, Samuel, and Henry N. Flynt. *Frontier of Freedom*. Hastings House. New York. 1952.
Chamberlain, Samuel. *Open House in New England*. Stephen Daye Press. Brattleboro, Vt. 1937.
Chamberlain, Samuel. *Portsmouth, New Hampshire*. Hastings House. New York. 1940.
Congdon, Hubert. *Old Vermont Houses*. A. A. Knopf. New York. 1946.
Downing, Antoinette, and Vincent Scully. *The Architectural Heritage of Newport, Rhode Island*. Harvard University Press. Cambridge, Mass. 1952.
Downing, Andrew J. *Cottage Residences*. Wiley & Putnam. New York. 1844.
Fowler, Orson. *A Home for All*. Fowler & Wells. New York. 1856.
Langdon, William C. *Everyday Things in American Life*. 1607-1776. Charles Scribner's Sons. New York. 1937.
Morrison, Hugh. *Early American Architecture*. Oxford University Press. New York. 1952.
Pickering, Ernest. *Homes of America*. Thomas Y. Crowell Company. New York. 1951.
Pratt, Richard. *A Treasury of Early American Homes*. McGraw-Hill Book Company, Inc. New York. 1949.
Robinson, Ethel, and Thomas Robinson. *Houses in America*. Viking Press. New York. 1949.
Saylor, Henry H. *Bungalows*. Robert M. McBride & Company. New York. 1909.
Stickley, Gustav. *Craftsman Homes*. Craftsman Publishing Company. New York. 1927.
Tallmadge, Thomas T. *The Story of Architecture in America*. W. W. Norton & Company, Inc. New York. 1927.
Waterman, Thomas T. *The Dwellings of Colonial America*. University of North Carolina Press. Chapel Hill. 1950.

Chapter XIII
The Problem of Taste

"Tell me where is fancy bred,
Or in the heart or in the head,
. . . .
It is engender'd in the eyes,
With gazing fed; and fancy dies
In the cradle where it lies."

The Merchant of Venice

Our ideas of what is desirable in dress, furnishings, and also in house design tend to change with the passage of time. For instance, the flat low rooflines of the ranch-style house that is now in fashion are pleasing to our eyes today, but back in the 1920's, when people were in love with the old English cottage, steep roofs were considered beautiful, and flat roofs looked unattractive. But if you go a little further back in time, to the bungalow era of about 1910, you will find that flat low roofs and wide eaves were popular then as they are now, and that the steep roof was out of favor.

Still another step back will take you to the tall narrow houses of the late Victorian period. Their steep Mansard roofs and long narrow windows show that vertical lines were popular then. Certain features of house design, such as the slope of the roof, the width of the eaves, emphasis on horizontal or vertical lines, and details of decoration, seem to swing in and out of fashion at intervals of twenty to fifty years.

Human nature being what it is, we can't help liking what is in fashion. While some feature of design enjoys public favor, it looks handsome, or at least acceptable, to our eyes. When the pendulum swings the other way, it goes out of style and we like it less. The simple dignified colonial houses of New England must have looked bare and barnlike to our Victorian grandparents, who loved jig-saw ornament and turrets and stained-glass windows. Bungalows looked squat and heavy to the home-builders of the 1930's, who were devoted to the dainty Cape Cod cottage. Perhaps the houses that we are building today with the best intentions in the world will make some future generation smile.

As the preceding chapter indicated, the history of architecture is the story of changes in design. The Gothic style followed the Romanesque, and in turn gave way to the classic forms of the Renaissance, because people liked different things at different times. The great style changes of history, however, are not the same thing as the artificially forced changes in house fashions of today, when modern methods of merchandising try to make us feel that our possessions are out of date before we have finished paying for them.

It is a pity that house design should be subject to rapidly changing fashion, but, if the experience of the past 100 years is any guide, there is one thing we can be sure of: the houses of today will some day look old-fashioned. There is very little we can do about that, but we can do something to keep them from looking ugly or silly.

Because it is difficult to look with an unbiased eye on the current fashions in houses, those of an older day are especially useful in developing standards of good design. If you study the houses in the older residential sections of your town you will find that some of them, even though they look old-fashioned, are still pleasing to the eye. We might not care to build new houses exactly like them, but we can give them respect and even admiration for their good design. Other houses, however, are both old-fashioned and ugly; if you analyze these latter houses, you will probably find that they have some of the following qualities:

1. A complex shape, and broken lines that have little or no relation to the structure of the plan.

2. Ultra-stylishness; in a Georgian colonial house it might mean a cornice that is too heavy and ornate, or an over-elaborate doorway. A house of picturesque type may have too steep a roof or be too dressy with imitation half-timber. It may have a conspicuous variety in the colors of bricks or roofing, or very rough stucco.

3. Clumsy design: bad proportion, such as dormers, porches, and gables that are too large for the size of the house; a lack of unity through too many different materials, or varying slants in the roof; a lack of balance through a grouping of all the main features of the house on one side, or a disorderly arrangement of windows that are too unlike in size, shape, and style to fit together.

On the other hand, those older houses that are still good to look at even though they are out of fashion, are likely to have the following qualities:

1. Honest design; a straightforward, logical structure, that bears a direct relation to the use of the space within. No false dormers or gables that do not add useful space, no unnecessary breaks in the roof line, no meaningless jogs in the walls.

2. Honest use of materials; no material is used as an imitation of something else; each material is used in a way that is consistent with its character.

3. Lack of pretentiousness; small houses do not pretend that they are mansions; large houses do not disguise themselves as cottages. Ornament, where it is used, is related to the structure, and is not excessive.

4. Design qualities, such as pleasing proportion of parts and details to the whole; orderly, balanced arrangement; unity of mass, color, and materials. Where two materials are used for the walls, they are related in character, and the change from one to the other is related in some logical way to the structure.

5. Another quality might be called architectural grace. It is hard to put your finger on it, because it is a subtle matter of design and feeling. It is the artistic talent of the architect shining through the wood and stone and brick. Talent is also an elusive quality. It includes mastery of design, a practical understanding of structure and materials, imagination and originality.

But talent in the architect may not be enough. If the owner's taste is bad, he may insist on having some feature of design that cancels out the architect's ability to create beauty. On the other hand, a client who knows something about good design can cooperate with the architect. By supplying an atmosphere favorable to creative work he can enjoy vicariously the satisfaction of producing a house that is a work of art.

Now any discussion of good taste means walking on thin ice. When we talk about developing taste, we imply that there is room for improvement. Such an implication does violence to an illusion we all cherish, namely, that our own taste is naturally perfect, or at least very good.

"Taste--critical judgment, discernment--is the most delicate fruit of learning and grows at the top of the tree. It ... is not, as is often supposed, the peculiar inheritance of gentle blood. It is the result only of study and critical observation."*

As Mr. Tallmadge defines the word, taste means judgment, which is based on thinking. "Taste" is also used quite often in a looser way, meaning someone's personal preferences. When we say, "That is not to my taste," we usually mean, "I don't like it." Now likes and dislikes are based mostly on emotional reactions. They have little or nothing to do with judgment, or thinking, unless one has acquired a good deal of knowledge on the subject involved. We are all inclined to confuse the two meanings of the word, and to assume that what we like must automatically be "good" taste, and that what we dislike must be inferior.

The practice of critical judgment calls for a tolerant attitude toward new and unfamiliar forms of design, and also toward the ideas of other people. Suspicion of the unfamiliar may be a natural inheritance from our primitive ancestors, but it may also act now to form a barrier to the development of taste.

A first step in the development of taste that is based on judgment instead of prejudice is to look for the reasons back of our likes and dislikes. When you say, "I don't like that house," ask yourself also, "Why don't I like it? Is it badly balanced, disorderly in arrangement, or lacking in unity? Are the materials honestly used, is the structure logical?" By thinking of design qualities as you look at houses, you can teach yourself to judge them as designs.

There are several guides to help us learn to think of houses in terms of design. The first of these is the work of the leading architects of the present day. They have spent years in the study of architectural design, and have had practical experience in planning houses. Naturally, they know more about houses than other people do, and fortunately, their work is available in books and magazines. It may not be possible to employ one of the best-known architects in the country to design your house, but is a comparatively simple matter to study the work he has done for others, and to learn something from it.

The second guide is also to be found in books and magazines. It is the houses of the past, here and in other countries. There is no better foundation for the development of good judgment in matters of taste than a well-developed historic back-

---

*Tallmadge, Thomas E. _The Story of Architecture in America._ W. W. Norton & Company, Inc. New York.

ground. It is difficult to be detached about houses (or furniture or clothes or motor cars) that are currently fashionable. We cannot help feeling that they look better than those products which have just gone out of style. But studying and appraising the designs of houses that were built so long ago that they no longer have any relation to current fashions will give you a long perspective on house design in general, and on today's houses in particular.

This does not mean that you should copy the houses of the past. We have come a long way from the feeling current in the 1920's, that a new house should be an authentic copy of a previous style period. Modern ways of living and new materials and techniques, plus the talent of modern architects, have produced the modern house. Creativeness, however, is not an exclusive possession of either the present or of the past. Talent, or the ability to create beauty, is as old as recorded history, and every age has had its talented builders. Beauty may be found in many different kinds of house, from the half-timber cottages of medieval England to the lacy marble facades of Venetian palaces. They are all available in books, and they are all yours to study and enjoy.

The two guides mentioned above imply a dependence for your taste on that of others, the builders of long ago and the architects of today. Such dependence can scarcely be avoided; as a layman, you must receive most of your ideas on houses second-hand, just as you receive your medical and legal ideas second-hand from your doctor and your lawyer. You will find, however, that you are growing more able to think for yourself as you study house design wherever you find it. To paraphrase Mr. Tallmadge's statement, your capacity for judgment will increase as you study and practice critical observation. Then, when you build your house, you will be able to avoid those faddish touches that so quickly "date" a house. Your house will eventually go out of fashion, no doubt, but you can always be proud of it if its design is good because good design is above and beyond fashion.

READING REFERENCES

Architectural Record. <u>Eighty-two Distinctive Houses</u>. F. W. Dodge Corporation. New York. 1952.
Creighton, Thomas. <u>Planning to Build</u>. Doubleday, Doran and Company. Garden City, New York. 1945.
Gloag, John. <u>Men and Buildings</u>. Chantry Publications Limited. London. 1950.
Hamlin, Talbot. <u>Architecture, an Art for All Men</u>. Columbia University Press. New York. 1947.
Hoynigen-Huhn, <u>Hellas</u>. J. J. Augustin. New York. 1943.
McGrath, Raymond. <u>Twentieth-Century Houses</u>. Faber and Faber, Ltd. London. 1934.
Pickering, Ernest. <u>Shelter for Living</u>. John Wiley and Sons, Inc. New York. 1941.
Progressive Architecture. <u>Homes</u>. Reinhold Publishing Corporation. New York. 1947.
Robsjohn-Gibbings, T. H. <u>Homes of the Brave</u>. Alfred A. Knopf. New York. 1954.

INDEX

Architect's services 7, 63

Basements 47
Bathrooms, plans 9
Bedrooms, arrangement 13
   minimum requirements 26
Building site, choice of 40
   planning 41
   rural 39
   sizes 36

Circulation 13
Classical architecture 68
Climate 43
Closets 13
Colonial houses 48, 73

Dining space, arrangement . . . 12
   area needed 13, 27
   out of doors 27
   part of living room 12
Doors, sizes 8
   hanging for best use of space . 8
   types 9

Elevations 19

Federal houses 76
Fireplace, location 11
   as shown on plan 9
   open three sides 11
   outdoor 28
French houses 72
Furniture, arrangement 8
   sizes 10

Gothic cathedrals 68
Greek Revival houses 76

Halls, entrance 16
   used as extra room 30
Half-timber 69

Kitchens, arrangement 22
   equipment sizes 22

Living room, arrangement 8
   division of 30

Medieval dwellings 69
   influence on American houses . 79
Model houses, judging 2
Modern houses, early 77
   their development 81

Orientation 36

Neighborhood, choice of 3, 40

Piano, placing of 12
Plans, copying 8
   judging 32
   relation to elevation 20
   relation to family 27
   shape in relation to cost . . . 16
Plumbing, economy in arrangement. 16
Porches 46

Renaissance Architecture 70
Romanesque Architecture 68
Roof, types 19
   overhang 45
Room sizes 15

Specifications 65
Split-level houses 51
Stairway, location 49
   planning 51
Storage wall 14

Tract houses 1
Traditionalism 79
Traffic lanes 11

Utility room 24

Victorian houses 76

Windows, as shown on plan . . . 9
   dormer 55
   high 21
   in elevations 19
   sizes 20